MW01064217

HOW TO FIND
Trouble Free Horse Boarding
Even if You Are New
to Horses

What you **MUST know, ask,** and **look for**
when searching for that *happy, safe* and
healthy home for your horse and
a *fun* place for you

Ronaye Ireland

How to Find Trouble Free Horse Boarding Even if You Are New to Horses

first edition

RONAYE IRELAND

Copyright © 2008 by Ronaye Ireland

Interior design: Ronaye Ireland
Cover design: Ronaye Ireland
Photography: Ronaye Ireland

Published by: Profits Publishing
http://profitspublishing.com

1300 Boblett Street
Unit A-218, Blaine, WA 98230
Phone: (866) 492-6623
Fax: (250) 493-6603

Notice of rights

All rights reserved. No part of this book may be reproduced or transmitted in any form or by any means, electronic, mechanical, photocopying, recording, or otherwise, without the prior permission of the publisher.

Notice of liability

The information in this book is distributed on an "as is" basis, without warranty. While every precaution has been taken in the preparation of this book, neither the author or the publisher shall have any liability to any person or entity with respect to any liability, loss, or damage caused or alleged to be caused directly or indirectly by the instructions contained in this book.

ISBN (10) - 1-933817-65-8
ISBN (13) - 978-1-933817-65-1

10 9 8 7 6 5 4 3 2

**In dedication to all the horses
who have touched my life and taught me
invaluable lessons.**

And to the horses who I will not meet...
But who, I know, will have better lives as a result of
the increased awareness in their owners.

Hi Wendy

Thank you for purchasing a copy of my book. I hope the information helps you the same way it has helped many others and their horses 😊

All the very best!

Love Ranaye.

Sep 16, 2016

Contents

PART ONE
Getting Started

PART TWO
Visiting the Facilities

PART THREE
Make Your Move

HOW TO FIND TROUBLE FREE HORSE BOARDING

Acknowledgements

And big hugs...

To my dear friend Sandra Draibye who has been a wonderful support throughout the whole process ...

To Jennifer Quazilbash ... talking about horses and boarding experiences takes much more than just an hour over dinner as we discovered when we closed down the pub!

To Jennifer Hannah ... who was new to horse ownership and took on self board right off the bat. That took a lot of guts Jen! Thank you for sharing your stories, your experiences and observations while helping me out with the evening feed.

To Sue Schulz from McFli's feedstore ... who was speechless after reading the first draft ... "You've got it all already!" Sue, the look on your face was priceless!

To Hermen Geertsema, DVM from Hermen Geertsema Equine Services ... my trusted vet who, with his crazy schedule, still managed to find the time to review my book.

To Kevan Garecki from H4 Services ... a long time and well respected hauler who has given me some excellent tips on what to look for when choosing a horse transport company.

To Kandys Anderson for lending me her eagle eyes proofreading and editing my book before turning it over to you.

To each of my boarders who have been patiently listening to me for months and given me their stories and insights.

To each of the contributors who responded to my posts sharing their frustrations, fears and the results they wanted when looking for a suitable home for their horse.

MANY THANKS to each of you.

Your help and positive feedback gives me the confidence that this book will be of great value to anyone looking for a trouble free horse boarding experience.

What Others Say About this Book

"This book gallops way ahead with author's knowledge and insight into the horse boarding world. Provided me with the most useful advice I've seen in a long time. Love for these animals comes through loud and clear. Four horseshoes way up!"

— *Carl Webster, Rural Farm Appraiser*

" 'How to find trouble free horse boarding, even if you're new to horses' is a long-overdue work of art! This book is a **must read** for all new horse owners and should be carefully considered by experienced horse people as well. It fairly teems with sagely advice and hard-earned wisdom that few of us could afford to discover on our own. I am very proud to have contributed in some small way to this endeavor."

— *Kevan Garecki, Professional Horse Hauler,*
H4 Services, www.h-4.ca

"Being a horse owner for the past 29 years, I can definitely say that I wish I had Ronaye's book beside me for some of those years when I needed to board my horse out. Thinking I had my horse's best interest in mind, I definitely went through my share of gut-wrenching challenges at many boarding facilities.

My horse got into turkey starter feed (someone didn't shut the gate properly behind them), barbed wire accidents (so bad that the vet thought she wouldn't make it through one) and unpredictable horse dynamics where she was getting hurt by being bullied more than a horse should, to name just a few of the problems.

Finding Ronaye's book, I realized that I can find the perfect stress-free board and have a healthy, mentally happy and safe horse. Ronaye runs her own boarding facility under the same concepts of her book.

By reading the many fantastic tips this easy-to-read book has to offer, you'll be thrilled to use it every step of the way in finding that safe and happy home your equine friend deserves!"

— Romana van Lissum,
A horse owner for almost 30 years, endurance rider for 6. Author of
How to be a Waitress and make Big Tips, www.HowToBeAWaitress.com

"I am soooooooooo happy I found your website and your fabulous book! I bought it right away. And I just had to write and thank you.

In a nutshell, I have rekindled my deepest passion – horses – now this late in my life. I couldn't be happier.

I realized when looking around for boarding near my home it wasn't just the 'vacancy' 'no vacancy' I had to be aware of. I can't thank you enough for all the information. Again I know it is easy to fall in love with these magical creatures but I have to be more than fiscally responsible too.

Your worksheets are going with me to every barn 'interview'. You are just a godsend! Brightest Blessings."

— Athyn, California, Horse Owner

"The book is extremely thorough without being boring. I love Ronaye's honesty and where she shares her moments being a newbie and lacked experience. There are even tips on what to look for when looking at roofing, how to spot potential problems and how these could be affecting your horse. Some of the information would never have crossed my mind. And it's not only about horses. There is also a large emphasis on helping you get a place that you enjoy.

Once you've read the book you really do feel prepared to find the perfect home for your horse and yourself. Before wasting time and money on a stable it would be well worth your while to read this first. You will definitely make fewer mistakes and have peace of mind knowing that you are doing the very best for your best friend, your horse.

I would love to read another informative book by Ronaye Ireland; she really speaks from experience and has a fun way of sharing what she has learned."

— Gail Nelson a newbie from Whonnock B.C.
Children's Math Games, www.PlatoLearn.com

"I wish Ronaye had written this book 12 years ago, when I first started boarding my horses. I realize now that I didn't have a clue of what to look for. Not till 8 years later, when I moved my horses to Ronaye's barn, did I find what I didn't know my horses and I needed. Since arriving, my horses have been well looked after, their stalls are always clean and comfortable, their food is customized to their needs, they have a fantastic turnout and pasture... but mostly, they are SAFE.

From the moment they arrived, they were relaxed – I couldn't believe how quickly they adjusted. Especially my mare – she's a very nervous horse who never wanted to leave the barn. In the 3 and ½ years we've been at Ronaye's, not once has Shady balked at going out to the pasture. In fact, she hates staying in her stall during the day. What a change!

Everything Ronaye has written in her book, she practices. She knows what she's talking about! Follow the advice she gives in this book – your horse will be happy and you will sleep soundly at night."

— Jo-Ann, Boarder at Jaquima Ranch

"... I've already been drawn in... It's very nicely designed (and that's a real compliment! I'm a book designer.) And your writing is friendly and inviting. The pictures add just enough interest, but aren't distracting. I'm amazed at all the details you've covered! You haven't missed a thing.

Also, it's really cool how you insert little stories along the way. Like the time your horse jumped out of the stall when snow slid off the roof and spooked her. I TOTALLY get it, like I was there with you! And your story about building your own round pen is very interesting. This is a fabulous book, and I'll recommend it to my friends."

— Liz Tufte, long time horse owner and boarder, Minneapolis, USA

"Thanks to your book, I recently found a GREAT barn for my horse! I knew which questions to ask and what to look for, and I didn't settle until I found exactly what I was looking for, in my budget. It took six visits, but I found the right one. My horse is happy and well cared for, and that makes me happy."

— Kim, Michigan, US

"I've boarded my horses for over thirty years and made many mistakes. Ronaye's thorough coverage of both sides of boarding (horse owner and barn owner) will give even a seasoned horseperson something to think about.

If you are going to board your horse, you really need to consider so much before turning your horse's care over to someone. Go through '**HOW TO FIND Trouble Free Horse Boarding, Even if You Are New to Horses**' and decide what you can compromise on and what you can't and take that list when you visit a barn.

If you're thinking of filling your barn with boarders, read the book first and find out if you really want to deal with all that goes with it. Every horse owner has their own idea of how things should be done and you will hear about it at some point. Ronaye's book will help anyone prepare for the well-being of their horse or their barn."

— Corinne Hunt, Canadian Holistic Pet Food, www.cdnholisticpet.com

"Whether you are a horse boarder or own a horse boarding farm, this book is a must read. Ronaye's research and first hand experience lays it all out in an easy, step-by-step manner so you can be sure to find the best boarding stable for your horse.

Before you choose the next home for your horse, take some lessons from Ronaye and make your choice with confidence!"

— *Marie Taulbee, Owner of LaRaedo Horse Farm Management Software, www.LaRaedo.com*

"Thanks Ronaye! You make what might otherwise be a dry subject come alive with your insights and the sharing of your vast field of experience. As a former cutting horse wrangler I've spent my time in and around the barn and you've proven to me again that you **can** teach an old dog new tricks..."

— *Liam Snell, In memory to Molly-Bee, my equine partner, www.OnTheWayToSantiago.com*

HOW TO FIND TROUBLE FREE HORSE BOARDING

Preface

1. My story

Ten years ago I had no idea what journey I was about to embark on when I decided to follow my passion for horses again.

At the time, I worked as a web developer and project manager in the IT department of an educational institution. I rented a little cabin in the midst of a forest and commuted an hour each way to work, joining the rest of the world in their daily existence.

As a young girl of eight in Holland, I was taught to ride horses using traditional English methods. In my late teens I lost interest, but apart from financial constraints and having to get a career going I was also really missing something in my relationship with horses.

Throughout the years I would ride off and on, but in 1999 the movie *The Horse Whisperer* created a real turning point for me.

I picked up the thread with horses again and started to learn about Natural Horsemanship with my green broke lease horse. This journey evolved into me buying my first three year old untrained horse a few years later.

I went through the entire experience of looking for a boarding stable and being a boarder before having my horses on my own property.

But the journey didn't stop there. My then husband and I bought the property with the intend of building a second house. In order not to lose the use of the first, we needed to get farm status.

Since I knew about horses, and rules to qualify for farm status now included the buying, training and selling of horses, we needed a barn. I could rent out a couple of stalls while I was at it!

Apart from an old riding arena, there was NOTHING here.

I spent months researching and designing the barn, paddocks, roadways and pastures, before we ever even broke ground.

My experience with the natural horsemanship made me very aware of what horses needed. My previous boarding experiences taught me about the things I liked and didn't like in a boarding stable. It also taught me about many safety aspects that typically got overlooked.

When I was looking around for board, I learned about the different boarding options available and what worked and didn't.

Buying my first horse taught me not only about the whole new world of horse ownership and the associated experience of dealing with the day-to-day care, vet and farrier visits but also the whole feeling of being a newbie.

Having a young untrained horse taught me about what I needed in support from instructors and training aids. And the list goes on. Everything I had touched in my journey with horses became a direct input for determining the layout of my property and my barn, and the set up of the boarding stable as a business.

But because I was building my barn from scratch, I put even that much more research and thought into every aspect of the usability and efficiency of the barn, the ease of cleaning, maintenance, the safety aspects, the well being of the horses, the needs of the vet and farrier, hay trucks and other service vehicles that needed to visit the facility.

I can tell you, not much got missed and my boarders, vet and farrier will attest to that.

When we finally broke ground I figured the barn was going to be finished in three to four MONTHS. Two YEARS later, I finally finished the barn to the point where I could open up for business.

While I still had my regular full-time job, I did all the costing, ordering of materials, organizing the trades and even worked alongside them.

I designed and redesigned a lot of the barn hardware used in and around my barn for the purposes of efficiency and safety.

▼ *The barn six months after breaking ground. I had NO idea how many more months of work there were ahead of me.*

I never thought I'd learn about framing, electrical or plumbing. I had to be an "expert" at just about everything even if it was just to make sure that the "professionals" did their job right!

So many times I had to crawl back in and redo the work they did because they made a mess out of things. It's "just a barn" people kept saying. My answer never changed, "It's not **just** a barn, it's MY barn." Get used to it!

It's now been five years since I first set foot on this property. The place has been transformed, though I'm certainly not done yet.

I have my farm class, three mares for breeding, one horse I use for lessons, one who is my riding horse, and one to be sold. The barn is full with ten boarded horses and I have two part-time employees. I train horses and teach people about natural horsemanship.

And now, I've even written a book... **this** book!

If you had told me ten years ago that this is what my life was going to look like, I NEVER would have believed you!

Let's focus on this book for a minute. **Why** did I write this book?

Part of my screening process for my boarders is that I visit their horses. Not only do I get to meet the horse, I also get to see the conditions in which they have to live. I have been appalled with some of the things I've seen and how unsafe or unfriendly some places are for horses.

I also hear about a lot of the frustrations and fears people have and why they are looking around for a better home.

When people visit my place, I notice how much gets overlooked. I have seen how unprepared people are when they buy a new horse and how little they actually know about what horses really need.

I have also seen how frustrated people are when looking for a boarding stable for their horse and I can so relate because I've been there!

As you've figured out by now, I have a very unique perspective.

Not only have I been the uninformed boarder and new horse owner, I have also built a complete boarding stable right from scratch, that includes designing the environment for the horses and also the business side of things of the actual running of the stable.

I have walked both sides of the fence for considerable miles.

As I talk about experiences and relay my stories within the book you'll find me switching back and forth between my times as a boarder and my role as a barn owner. The two perspectives are vastly different, and each with their associated challenges.

Just as much we as boarders have our frustrations with how places are run, the reverse is also true. We barn owners are just as much up against the wall when trying to balance the needs of the horses, the individual requirements of the boarders and the incredible cost, time and energy required to run the facilities.

My goal with this book is to help minimize the frustrations and fears you feel when trusting the care of your horse to a total stranger.

This book will raise your awareness of what horses really need to be happy and give you the tools and confidence to make the right decision for your horse the first time around.

I also want to raise your awareness on how accepted business practices can affect your horse and you in negative and positive ways.

I will be giving you lots of questions you can ask and things you should look for so you don't have to "learn" these through trial and error, expensive vet bills and multiple moves.

Even if you're contemplating getting a horse for the first time, the information in this book will help you sift through the different aspects of this whole new world of horse ownership.

So, please use this book to guide you when looking for that HAPPY, SAFE and HEALTHY HOME for your horse and a FUN place for you!

After all, owning a horse should be a BLISSFUL journey.

Wouldn't you agree?

2. Your story

You just came home from the barn frustrated and upset. It's pouring cats and dogs out there and you just watched your dear horse huddled on one side of her stall with the rain just pouring in through the roof on the other side. She's standing in soggy manure and bedding and the winter has only just begun. For the entire summer, the barn owner had promised that the roof was going to be fixed but nothing ever came of it.

~

Your horse has been putting on far too much weight and after numerous talks with the barn owner your horse is still not moved off the grass. You're worried about founder since your last horse suffered for three years with this and you don't want to go through it AGAIN.

~

You've asked your horse to be put next to another horse so he's not so anxious and stops running along the fence. After all, he needs a buddy and doesn't like to be by himself. The barn owner insists on keeping your horse separate and well away from the others because he feels the horse is unruly and dangerous, not realizing that his decisions are making the situation only worse.

~

The paddocks are in such disrepair that the barn owner has had to close them down for the winter months. There are 30 horses in the barn and only 12 functioning paddocks. Horses are rotated in and out but barely get more than an hour a day to stretch their legs. A year later, the paddock situation still hasn't been resolved.

~

A new facility has just opened up their doors and has room for 60 horses. The facility is located on 3.5 acres and has two outdoor arenas and one indoor plus the barn on the same 3.5 acres. Horses are stuffed together like sardines.

~

You just received a phone call from the barn owner letting you know that your horse got into the turkey feed and could you please come down.

~

You show up at the barn to find your horse's feet completely cut up by barb wire fencing. You didn't get a call. And this isn't the first time either.

~

The barn sports a policy that ALL horses must be tied in the cross ties. Your horse already slipped and went down once. Luckily no one was hurt. Safety clips were rusty and non-functioning. Knives were nowhere to be found. You and your horse definitely have different ideas about the safety of cross ties.

~

You show up at the barn around feeding time and find rats feeding out of the same bucket as your horse.

~

You show up at a barn only to find all the water buckets and troughs empty. You don't even board there but end up filling them up anyway.

~

Your reasons for looking for a new boarding stable will be unique to you. Perhaps you're new to horse ownership or you've decided to sell your property but don't want to give up on your horses. Or you're simply not happy anymore with the current conditions and circumstances.

But regardless of how different your reasons for moving may be, the journey of finding a new home will be very similar.

So, let's get started...

1

PART ONE
Getting Started

Chapter 1
Preparing for Your Search

When I bought my first horse, a beautiful three year old Tobiano paint (no bias here!). I was boarded at a private full-board facility. Apart from trail access and an outdoor arena there wasn't anything else. I really wanted to have access to a round pen seeing that my new boy was just halter broke and had never seen a saddle let alone a rider.

At that time I didn't know much about training a horse that basically knew nothing, but I had just started attending the local Parelli clinics, so figured I should be ok.

In the past I had been using some of the techniques I learned from Doug Mills and Monty Roberts plus I had worked with a trainer who had taught me lots about working with my lease horse when he was just five and barely broke. So, I didn't enter this deal entirely blind, though blind I was as I certainly learned!

I didn't really want to move away from the barn where I boarded, but the round pen was high on my list so I decided to check out a few places. When I made my calls I had no idea what I was looking for, apart from the fact that the facility was to have a round pen.

That's when I learned about self and semi board. I also learned that with my work schedule these weren't going to be very workable options for me.

At one place, I quite liked the barn owner but felt uncomfortable with the rest of the people that were hanging out there. I also felt awkward with where they wanted to put my horse for the night. It wasn't bad, but just very different from what my boy was used to.

With this being such a new journey for me, I felt intimidated as well. I was surrounded by all these "savvy" horsey people. I lived in a sub-division and didn't really know what horses needed.

In all, this whole visit was quite an education for me. It made me realize that I really didn't know what was out there, but more so, what did I really want for myself and my horse? How did I want him to live? What kind of people did I feel comfortable with?

This experience certainly taught me that I needed to do some soul searching before picking up the phone...

1. What different styles of boarding are there available?

There are five styles of boarding that I'm aware of: Pasture, self, semi, full and all inclusive board.

However, just because boarding stables may give their boarding options the same name doesn't mean that they actually include the same services or carry the same expectations. So, you'll need to check this out carefully, but first let's find out what some of the variations are so that you can get a rough idea of what might be for you.

Pasture Board

This is the least expensive option and if you have an easy keeper, and that means a horse that is hardy and comfortable staying out all the time, this may be an option for you.

With pasture board, feed and water should be included. When a professional boarding stable offers pasture board then this will likely be the case. But some places will just give you a field and you take care of the rest. Other places may require you to supply the feed as it's not included in the price but they will do the feeding for you.

If you're doing pasture board in the hope to save on feed, you better check out the quality and quantity of grass available. And if you're hoping for your horse to live on grass alone during the summer months, you will need to pay close attention to the size of the field and the quality of the grass.

How much land you would need for one horse I can't tell you since there are so many variables to consider. For instance the type and quality of the soil will determine what kind of grass and how much of it will grow.

Clay soils hold a lot more moisture and is much more "grass friendly" then rocky soils that have difficulty holding the water.

Where you live also plays a big factor. In my area, where I get lots of rain, you may be alright with two acres for one horse, but in drier climates it could be as much as four acres per horse. And, of course, if the fields are poorly maintained you'll need a much larger area as well. So, make sure you pay attention to the size of the field.

And here are some other things… could you put down an electric fence if you wanted to, so you can split the field in two to have the ability to rest one part while your horse is on the other grazing? Is there too much grass? Could your horse founder? Is there a sacrifice area – area without grass, like a paddock or dirt patch – where you could put him to control how much he eats? Would they move him for you?

If the pasture doesn't provide enough food for your horse, will extra feed be supplied? If you are to rely on the grass, will the owners harrow and reseed the fields with descent forage? It's my hunch they won't. Maintaining good grazing fields is labor intensive and expensive and would cost more than the money they'd receive for board.

What about a companion for your horse? Are there other horses that he will be sharing the field with or is he going to be all by himself? Some horses do ok by themselves, but as a rule, horses should not be left without herd buddies. And if there are pasture buddies, would they make suitable companions for your horse?

The pasture should also have a proper run in shelter for your horse where he can get out of the weather. With some pasture board, they expect your horse to rely on trees. That's fine perhaps if they're evergreens with a good canopy underneath them where the horses can hide. But not so cool if the trees lose their leaves in the winter time and leave no shelter for the horses. So be aware of the seasons!

Just because it looks acceptable now doesn't mean it will at another time of the year.

Since this is a pretty bare bones option of boarding, you may not have access to many amenities or the use of any facilities, like an arena for example.

Things to Consider ...

— *Do I expect my horse to live on grass alone? If yes, then the the **size** of the field, and the **quality** and **quantity** of grass matters.*

— *Would I be okay with my horse having trees for shelter or do I need a proper shelter?*

— *Do I have the time to see my horse twice a day?*

— *Do I need to have the feeding and daily fresh water taken care of by the property owners?*

— *Is my horse prone to founder?*

— *Are amenities important?*

— *Do I want to have access to any facilities?*

— *Does my horse need a sacrifice area?*

— *Would I want to share with someone else so that my horse could have a buddy?*

— *Do I have any say in who that buddy is?*

— *What happens if a very dominant horse is being introduced or the two horses simply don't get along?*

Self Board and Semi Board

I'm including these two under the same heading since these terms seem to get interchanged a lot. So it can get a little confusing.

Self board means that you are given a space to keep your horse. That may include a paddock, or access to a pasture, for daily turnout and a stall. You may also have access to the facilities like an arena, a round pen, or even a public washroom, so if you have the available time to take care of the chores; this may be an economical option for you.

However, make sure you do the math! With self board it is your responsibility to buy his feed and take care of the daily cleaning, feeding and turn in and turn out for your horse. Some places may also require you to purchase your own bedding.

Semi board is pretty much the same with the exception that there could be an arrangement where the barn owner will feed your horse in the mornings provided that you've prepared all his food the night before. They will also turn him out for you.

This was the arrangement offered to me at the place where I looked. In all not a bad deal actually. Considering I had a full time job and it was on my way home, this could have worked quite well for me. With my crazy commute at times, mornings were a bad time for me to be running out to the barn so having someone else take care of my boy in the morning was quite appealing.

With self board, people tend to team up and share the duties. This works well when people pull their weight and have similar philosophies about handling but it becomes a real problem very quickly when people don't. What if you are well organized and always make sure that you have enough bedding, feed and hay for your horse and the other is always late in getting their supplies? What are you going to do? Let the other horse go hungry? Leave him in a filthy stall? The horse suffers, not the owner.

Very quickly people that don't pull their weight will take advantage of those that do. Short of complaining to the barn owner and hope they will tap into their position of authority, there isn't much you as an individual can do. It's their horse.

This for me was a very big reason why I decided to offer full-board only and not touch self or semi board. I didn't want to see horses living in dirt or go hungry.

Neither did I want to see horses fed at wildly different times. "They just got their dinner, but what about me, can't I have mine too?" Your horse doesn't understand!

As a barn owner, I'm quick to see the nightmares and the added complexities in managing people because ultimately, my neck is on the line.

But more so, I simply love horses too much. Horses have given up their freedom involuntarily and we've made them dependent on us. And yet, in their captivity they prove to be an incredibly loyal friend. It is now up to us to live up to our end of the deal and give them what they need. Is that so much to ask for? Unfortunately, for some people it is.

Another challenge is having other people handle your horse the way you'd like to see him handled. Just because you are kind and fair to your horse doesn't mean that another will be.

One of my boarders was just telling me stories of how one lady at her previous boarding place used to whack my boarder's horse over the head every time he was a little pushy or would nip. "That's how you deal with this kind of behavior", her co-boarder would say. Whenever this lady would enter the barn my boarder's horse would tense right up. That's a bad sign and why is that necessary? He was just a troubled four year old boy who had a rough start in life and needed someone he could trust so he could feel safe. He's a phenomenal horse with a big kind heart.

One last thing that you need to be aware of is that you are likely to run into places that offer self board for the purpose of getting some extra money for the use of their barn and grass fields, however, they have no intention of being involved with the care of your horse.

This being the case, there is a good chance that they have no experience with horses either and therefore don't understand how horses live and behave. They may get upset with you because the horse eats the fences, or turns the grass into a mud hole. But worse, they may not know to keep their kids from tearing through your horse's field with their mountain bikes. See, it's their property and they can do what they want, at least so the thinking goes.

I would not feel comfortable leaving my horse in a situation like this. My preference would be a self board situation where the property owners have a genuine interest in horses and at least have basic handling skills and enough knowledge to recognize a problem.

This doesn't mean that self and semi board can't work well. The barn owner has a big responsibility in making sure that the place runs properly and that horses are cared for. If supplies run out and I wasn't aware of it, I'd appreciate a quick call from my pal or the barn owner to remind me. Strict barn rules and good management can help the success of the place. And much of what I cover later on applies for self or semi board just the same.

Here are some things for you to take into consideration though while you're pondering self or semi board versus other options.

I think foremost is your available time. Even though you may be able to set up a buddy system with another boarder, you have to prepare yourself for the worst case scenario and ask yourself: "Can I attend to my horse in the morning hours and evening hours, seven days a week, 365 days per year, to make sure that his needs are taken care of?"

Second is your proximity to the barn. The closer you live, the easier it is to quickly "pop over". The further away your horse lives, the more difficult it becomes. If he is on your way to work, but 20 minutes away from your home, what happens when you're sick or on holidays? Those 20 minutes suddenly could become the reason why you won't go. What about attending to medical issues? You don't necessarily have a resource available that you could pay to take care of your horse while you might be unavailable.

Check with the barn owner whether or not there is a backup system in place that you can tap into in case you can't make it. Are they at all even involved with what is going on with the horses on their property? Some self board facilities don't want anything to do with the care of the horses, that's why they offer self board. It's all up to you. So, what happens if a horse gets sick? How will you be notified?

Now I'd like you to step outside for a moment and take a good look at your car. Could you see it loaded with hay bales, feed bags and supplements? How much can you transport? Do you have a roof rack? How far do you have to travel and how often in the week would you have to make the trip to the feed store? Are you prepared to live with the mess it makes of your car? If you have no means of transporting the feed, do you have any other options you can explore? Hauling hay around in your Volkswagen Bug could be quite entertaining, and not just for you!

Often we're attracted to self or semi board options because of cost. The initial price sounds less but that's why it's so important to find out what is included and what is not and to work out the math. And don't forget that driving time is an important part of this equation too.

See, one of the attractive things about offering self and semi board from the facility's perspective is that the barn owner removes themselves from the ongoing price increases of hay, grain, bedding and labor. Instead they leave it up to you to deal with. And that's not necessarily a bad thing. Whenever a barn has to put up their prices, boarders don't tend to receive the increases with smiling faces and without objections and that's not much of a fun thing to deal with.

Things to Consider ...

— *What will the barn owner do in case someone doesn't take care of their horse properly?*

— *Is there a group of people that you can buddy up with to share the duties?*

— *Is there is a backup system in place that you can tap into in case you can't make it?*

— *Are the owners of the property at all involved with what is going on with the horses on their property?*

— *Are kids running around in the fields where the horses are housed?*

Full Board

This was the option that best suited me at the time when my job took me into town and required me to drive over an hour each way. I always felt there was something missing though. Sometimes I felt that the barn owner had a better relationship with my horse than me. But now with my horses living at home, there are times when I think back fondly of the freedom full board actually gave me.

There certainly are big benefits in being involved with your horse's daily care. It builds that stronger bond, but your time spent feeding, cleaning, and getting the groceries cuts into your available time that you could spend riding or doing other fun things with him.

With full board feeding, cleaning, turning in and out plus the use of the facilities are all included. Some facilities may also include blanketing, fly masks on/off and basic medical care.

If you have a busy schedule or a career that takes you out of town, then this makes a lot of sense. Make sure you check out carefully what is included and what is not though.

I have heard of one instance where feed and bedding were not included with full board which really surprised me. The owner was required to purchase and supply these while the barn owner would take care of all the other needs like cleaning, feeding and turnout. In this case, the barn owner would not contact the owner when supplies were low and neither did the owner of the horse ever show up to check on her horse. It was one of the self boarders that would take it upon herself to let the owner know that she needed to get bedding or that she had run out of hay! How crazy is this?

If you're going for full board, make sure that at least your feed and bedding are included. Feed and bedding are consumables and some horses simply need and use more. If your horse happens to be one of those, don't be surprised if the barn sends you a monthly bill for the extras.

Some places may include a full blanketing service and others may only include X number of blanket changes or none at all. Blanketing is a very time consuming activity especially if a horse chooses not to cooperate.

Basic medical care may or may not be included. Scheduling and standing for the vet and farrier are generally not included either, but some places do. As you can see, it's important to figure out exactly what "full board" means.

All Inclusive Care

I know that when I bought my first horse, I made a clear commitment to him that he'd be with me until the day he dies. There may come a point in my life where I suddenly find that I can't physically take care of him, but that doesn't mean he would have to be sold and leave my care. An all inclusive care solution might just be the answer for me at that time.

All inclusive care would include the things that are typically offered with full board like feeding, cleaning and turnout but would also include the organization of regular vet and farrier appointments, blanketing, fly mask service, basic medical care and weekly or bi-weekly grooming sessions. In some cases the cost of farrier trims will be included and even basic vet care.

The idea is that ALL your horse's needs are taken care off while you can't be there for extended periods of time. I've even heard of people sending their horses off to different continents to give their horses that special retirement.

As part of the package, you should be getting regular updates on how your horse is doing and now with the ease of the internet and digital photos, there is no reason for you not to be getting a few pictures as well.

2. Which boarding style is for you?

Cost of board is often the first item on our list – I know it was for me. But the real question to ask yourself is whether or not you want to be involved with the day to day care of your horse. If your answer is yes and you're considering self board there are a whole bunch of other things that come into the picture.

If you're new to horses it can be a steep learning curve if you decide to take on self board. You may have lots of riding and handling experience, but taking on the full responsibility of the care of a horse is a different story.

This was certainly the case for me, except I didn't do self board; instead my horses came to live with me at home. I guess that's as good as self board.

I certainly had my share of questions and uncertainties. How do I figure out what and how much I should be feeding my horses, what about veterinary and farrier care? Where do I buy feed and hay? How do I decide what feed is right when there are so many choices? What if I make a mistake; will I know what to do in case something goes wrong?? Who would I call? How do I know when I'm overdoing something?

Getting overwhelmed yet?

I have to admit, it was kind of scary but entertaining at the same time. I know my horses had a few good laughs at my expense – "hey rookie!"

It's also a life style that we have to adopt and only you can decide whether you're willing and able to commit yourself 7 days a week 365 days per year, cleaning and feeding twice per day.

And that's not all of it. There is also the running around to pick up feed and supplies. Do you have a car that can accommodate the hay that you have to haul? You need to organize your vet and farrier visits and be there when they come to the barn. Could you share the duties with other boarders? It's a good idea to ask the barn owner whether people are into this kind of thing and whether there may be a group you could tap into.

Can you afford the time it takes? Are there things that would have to fall by the way side if you took on the care of your horse? How much time can you really commit to your horse comfortably? How far away from the barn do you live? Do you have other family commitments that could prevent you from going to the barn? What about holidays and Christmas time? What about work commitments? Does your work require you to travel for extended periods of time? Do you often get hit with last minute deadline related requests at work that can't wait and require you to stay late?

If owning a horse is new to you, you will need others around you that have experience. You'll want a support system that helps you win rather than one that puts you down.

One of my boarders was in this situation. She was regularly told that she didn't know what she was doing, but no one reached out to show her the way either. They just pointed fingers. It certainly didn't help her confidence in any way, shape or form.

When you're new to horse ownership you can't tell right from wrong. You haven't built up an experience base yet from which you can draw to make your own decisions. Therefore it's important that you feel good about the barn owner and the people who board at the facility because you need people around you that will enable you rather than disable you. Check with the barn owner too, to see if they're willing to help you through until you build up your confidence to do it on your own.

So, ask yourself:

— *Do I WANT to take care of my horse day after day in the first place?*

If YES,

— *Do I have the available time it takes?*

— *What and when are my current commitments?*

— *Would my work schedule interfere?*

— *What about family commitments?*

— *What about holiday time?*

— *When am I able to get to the barn?*

— *What kind of arrangement would I need to have in place in order for it to work?*

— *How far is the barn away from my home?*

— *Can I transport the necessary supplies?*

3. What can you afford and where are some of the hidden costs?

Horses are expensive... I sure found that out in a hurry. And it has nothing to do with the purchase price. That's the easy part!

It's everything after the fact. Now we need halters, saddles, rain sheets, winter blankets, fly masks, grooming aids, you name it. He needs manicures and doctor's appointments. For most of us we also need to rent a one bedroom apartment for him; it's just not that practical to have him share the couch at home like a cat or dog, though some people do it.

When you start adding it all up the expenses could run as high as those for a single person living on their own.

I used to rent a one bedroom apartment for $450 per month. If you go for full board, it could cost you more than that. If you want access to a gym, you pay an extra $100 each month for membership. To have access to an indoor arena or ring, you typically pay an extra $100 per month around here.

And what about memberships, events, clinics, and other fun stuff?

This is an expensive hobby, plain and simple. So putting a budget together is very important, but it's also very important to build in some breathing room so that you can accommodate board increases and possible surprises like unforeseen vet bills.

Self and semi board provides you with the basic space your horse needs: a stall, turnout area and an area where you can store your things.

Oh, and while I think of it, be sure that the barn has the basic needs like manure forks and wheel barrows! As well, the more you can store at the barn the fewer trips you have to make to the feed store. Apart from pasture board, this may be the most economical option just because you are taking care of the labor portion.

However, we now need to add in the extras and see if it still is an economical solution.

So, here are some of the basics that you'll need to include:

— *Hay*

— *Grain and salt*

— *Bedding (some places may have this included)*

— *Supplements*

— *Travel*

  ▪ *Distance to the feed store*

  ▪ *Number of visits per week to the feed store*

  ▪ *Distance to the barn (from your home, from your work)*

  ▪ *Number of visits to the barn per day*

— *Cost of gas for the above travel*

— *Make a note of the amount of time you'll be spending in the car driving around ... your time is worth something too you know.*

With *full board* you don't have to worry about all the things we just talked about with self and semi board. You don't need to be at the barn every day or make regular trips to the feed store, but if you live in town you may decide to move your horse further out so that he can have access to better turn out. Now instead of being 5 minutes away from the barn, you may be an hour away. So, make sure your travel time and gas expenses are part of your budget, especially with the constant rise in gas prices.

As we've already seen, full board can have different meanings so it's very important to be clear on what is included and what is not.

In my mind, full board should at minimum include a shelter, turn out, feed and feeding, fresh water, bedding and cleaning. Beyond this you get into the "extra services" domain and some may be part of the package and others may not. Or they may be included, but up to a certain point like blanketing for example. This may surprise you, but blanketing can quickly become a very time consuming task.

I have a couple of horses where sometimes I'm switching evening blankets for day time blankets. Sometimes it's double blankets or in the summer time I have to put fly sheets on for the day, off for the night. The amount of time involved with this many changes add up very quickly, so it's understandable that there will be restrictions or extra fees.

Extra bedding and feed obviously will be dependent on what your horse actually uses. And what your horse needs will be largely dependent on breed and what you do with him.

If you're new to horse ownership see if the barn owner can give you a rough ballpark of what your horse might need for food based on their past experiences.

Following is a list of things that may or may not be included and if not included they will be candidates for optional extra charges. On the flip side, there are going to be some things that won't be included, but you will be required to do them, like deworming and certain vaccines for example.

You will also want to check on the "barn rate" since services like standing for the vet for example will be based on that.

So, here are some of the likely candidates that could be subject to extra charges:

— *Extra bedding*

— *Extra feed*

— *Deworming*

— *Fly masks on/off in the summer months*

— *Fly spray*

— *Blanketing in the winter time*

— *Blanketing in the summer time (fly sheets, rain sheets)*

— *Bandaging*

— *Grooming*

— *Basic medical care like attending to cuts and scrapes*

— *Basic medical supplies*

— *Medical care when your horse is sick and you can't be there*

— *Medicating*

— *Supplements*

— *Adding supplements to the feed*

— *Standing for the Vet*

— *Standing for the Farrier*

— *Organizing Vet and Farrier appointments*

— *Pasture turnout*

In addition to the above, you also have to allow for veterinarian and farriery care. Give yourself some extra room here too in case your horse becomes ill or injured. Vet bills are NOT cheap.

If you're into shows and competitions you'll want to include entry fees, hauling fees, and travel expenses for example. Perhaps you

---

need to train your horse and need the help of a trainer? If you want to take lessons, you'll need to add those to the budget.

What about things for your horse like blankets, grooming aids, tack, etc? When you're on a budget you really have to set some boundaries on this, because it's way too much fun and easy to buy things for your horse.

So, let's see what we've got:

— *Distance and travel time to the barn*

— *Gas expenses to get to and from the barn*

— *Vet visits (2x per year for general care)*

— *Farrier visits (6x per year on average)*

— *Laundry service for blanket cleaning*

— *Memberships to clubs*

— *Subscriptions to magazines*

— *Insurance*

— *Entry fees for shows*

— *Pony club fees*

— *Clinics*

— *Hauling fees to get to clinics or shows*

— *Truck and trailer maintenance*

— *Travel expenses*

— *Training for your horse*

— *Lessons for you*

— *Blankets, tack, fly masks, halters, etc. for your horse*

— *Grooming aids*

— *Supplements (these are rarely included with board)*

And I have no doubt that you have some more things that you could add to this list.

Now, tally up your expenses for the year and then divide that by 12 months. That will give you your monthly budget that you need for your horse.

Can you afford it?

There will be times of the year when expenses will be higher and other times when expenses will be lower. Summer time is usually the most active time of the year when it comes to riding and showing. So you may have to balance your budget so that you will have the necessary funds available for the things you want to do during these more active times.

4. What makes a good home for your horse?

For me it's very important that my horses get to live like horses. They need the safety of the herd, the social interactions, play mates, and the ability to move around. Within the constraints of available space on my ten acres I've done my best to provide a happy, safe and healthy home for the horses that live here.

My horses are very quiet, content and have plenty of play drive. I don't have problems with colic, lameness or other health related issues that we often see in horses who are put in small confined areas for long periods of time. My horses are always curious and interested in what goes on around them. I never have a stiff or crabby horse to deal with when I do ground work or take them out for a ride. And there are times I don't do anything with them for six months and sometimes more – including my Thoroughbreds. None of the horses on the property exhibit any of the stress related vices either.

A good home that's stimulating and allows your horse to move around is very important. His contentment and well being doesn't only transfer directly into your relationship with him, but also in his performance as an athlete.

Finding a boarding solution that meets both your needs and those of your horse isn't going to be an easy task. Most boarding stables are built with you in mind first. After all, you pay the board and you make the decisions. A boarding stable also has big bills to pay and the more horses and people they can have stay at their barn, the easier it is to make ends meet and keep prices at more affordable levels for you.

If barns were built by horses you wouldn't see horses in box stalls and in tiny paddocks. I'd even doubt you'd find a wash stall, let alone an arena! You would find large fields with good solid shelters, a mud pool and a bunch of trees for the local hang out.

Age and Compatible Mates

Having watched the horses here on the property and spending the time building compatible and happy herds, I've certainly learned that the age of a horse is a big consideration.

A young horse needs other young horses to play with, but he also needs adults around to teach him about herd socials and to give them a sense of security. I had a 2 year old come live with us and since I already had a 2 and a 3 year old, it made sense to put the three together.

What was very interesting to watch is that the responsibility to look after the two 2-year olds was too much for the 3-year old even though he took on the role of leadership because he felt he needed to. He was simply too young and so not ready to take on this level of responsibility. He still needed to be a kid as well. When I put the three "kids" together with my two adult boys, the 3-year old was suddenly so much happier and so were the other two boys – they no longer got "picked" on. My two "uncles" made sure the youngsters were taken care of and allowed to be kids. It all made far too much sense.

If you have an older horse that doesn't move around so much anymore you also need to look at who they'd be "hanging out" with. Older horses don't mix so well with the younger ones. They just don't have the energy any more. They much prefer to hang out in the barn where it's cool and fly free.

My barn is quite flexible and I can combine the stalls as I see fit. I have three mares that are very close in age (28, 30 and 34), and they love the fact that I can combine their three stalls and two paddocks.

In fact, one of my boarders laughed when she saw the arrangement and said it was like they had a three bedroom apartment with a couple of patios. There are times of the day where these old gals much prefer to be sitting in a rocking chair staring off in to the distance mulling over the past than playing a game of tag.

If your horse is kind of in the middle, it's easier to put him in with others.

But before I continue on, let's talk for a minute about easy keepers vs. hard keepers.

Typically easy keepers are considered those that are hardy and don't require a lot of food or special care like blanketing. The flip side is a hard keeper. They need a lot of food, lose weight easily and require a lot of extra care.

However, an easy keeper can be a hard keeper. Ok... so how is that?

A horse may not require a lot of food, blanketing or any other special care. But he may be an individual that's very curious and needs a lot of stimulation. He may also be dominant and very food oriented which prevents him from being turned out with other horses because he'll eat all their food. If he's bored, he'll start to

▼ *The "over 30" crowd enjoys the flexibility of the barn.*

chew on stuff like there is no tomorrow. Or if he's in the herd and he happens to be bored he'll start to chase the other horses for pure entertainment. He's moody and pissy because his needs aren't met.

If you were to put this kind of a horse in a box stall and a small paddock you'd have the potential of ending up with a dangerous beast on your hands. In my books – that's a far cry from an easy keeper. And, yes, I live with a horse that's like this and the owner and I have managed to find a balance. It's working but I'm not entirely convinced that it's ideal.

Think about your horse for a minute. Make a note of your horse's age and temperament. What do you think he would need in terms of companions? What is his personality like? Is he very dominant, aggressive, or submissive? Does he favor mares or geldings? Are there certain types of horses that he should never be turned out with? If he's young, would you like him to be with other youngsters?

Handling

When you board out your horse, other people will be handling him. I know for me that's a big one. I really don't want to see my horse being mishandled or handled roughly. I also follow the principles of Natural Horsemanship and would much prefer handlers who do the same. Since this is very close to my heart I would be looking for a barn that followed the same philosophy, and perhaps even style, as me. It's the only way I could ever see me being comfortable leaving my horse in someone else's care.

So, if you have a particular style or philosophy that you follow with your horse, or if there are styles or behaviors that you're absolutely not ok with, make a note of it. Be very clear on what you will and will not accept. This is something that you'll need to observe or chat about with the barn owner when you visit the facilities.

Stalls

My horse is pretty average, 15.2h, and is comfortable in a 12x12 stall. He would still be ok in a 10x10 but it's border line. If you have a very tall horse or a big warm blood you will not want anything smaller than 12x12 feet, especially if he's to be in there for extended periods of time. I've seen 17.2h Thoroughbreds in 10x10 stalls and it just is way too small.

Stallions need more than 12x12. I've seen 14x14 as a recommendation but a lot of barns are build with a spacing of 12 feet between supports, so 12x16 would give you the equivalent in square footage.

Make sure your horse can turn around. I have seen stalls that are 8 feet wide by 10 or 12 feet long. Fine for a pony perhaps but a long horse won't be so comfortable. Stalls come in many shapes and sizes so before you settle on a home for him make sure the stall is big enough.

Some barns have a variety of stall sizes. If that is the case, ask the barn owner which stall your horse is likely to be kept in. In most barns you will be assigned a stall for your horse.

However in some cases, as is in my case, horses don't get assigned to a stall. This was something my boarders really had to get used to. Since I have paddocks attached to my stalls and the horses are free to come and go as they please, it's about who gets along with whom.

When I have new horses come into the barn, I have to look for compatible fence mates and that sometimes requires me to move horses around. Once my boarders saw how it worked and realized that it was much safer that way, they were totally fine with it.

Turnout

Pasture turnout for me is the number one thing on my list for my horse, and it's not even about the grass. I know he loves to roam and play with herd mates. I also don't like to see my horse ever locked up. He hates it. So, for him a run in shelter, a large field and a bunch of herd buddies is all he needs.

I have a little Arab here, a feisty 30 year old gal, who's prone to colic if turned out on grass, so her owner requested that she'd have a stall and paddock.

What do you think your horse needs? Are there any medical conditions that could restrict where he's turned out? Can he only be out on grass during the day and not night?

Some horses just gain weight too easily and could be candidates for founder. If your horse is very energetic he will need more space than one who's pretty laid back or simply old. If paddocks were the only turnout available, what would be the minimum size your horse would need?

▼ *My boarder's little Arab enjoying her new home.*

5. What kind of care do you want your horse to have?

I'm thankful that my boy is an easy keeper and doesn't need a lot of special care. He rarely ever has a cut or scrape and is never lame. So if I had to put a list of things together that I would like to see included with board, my list would be pretty short.

Fly masks in the summer would be a definite and they would have to come off for the night. If he was cut or ended up with scrapes from a scrap in the herd, I'd want those to be at least checked and if necessary taken care of. They don't take much to do and would certainly prevent infection from setting in. If it was a deep cut, I'd want to be called about it. If he sprained a tendon, at least cold hose him and call me. In the winter time when it gets really cold, throw a blanket on or if it's non-stop rain for days, even with a shelter I'd still like to see him have a rain sheet. If we get a sunny day in the middle of a rain stretch, give him at least a break from the blanket. That's about it really.

If you had a horse that had moved from a hot and dry climate to a cold and wet climate, specific blanket requirements may be high on your list to help your horse acclimatize and deal with the colder temperatures. He has no built in system to protect him from the wet and cold and needs your help.

I have two ex-race horses from Hong Kong staying here. They came to Canada about three years ago and the owners told me that it was quite the adjustment for them. Since Hong Kong is humid and warm and 15 degrees is considered cold, the boys didn't grow a winter coat to protect them against the cold and wet conditions of our area. They had quite the blanketing routine to help them cope. And even now there will be times when they have one for the day time and another for night.

If you clip your horse during the winter months, you also have to compensate with blanketing since he won't have anything to keep him warm or protected from the rain and cold.

Your horse could have laminitis and require special care or perhaps he has Cushing's disease and needs medication added to his feed. If your horse is older, there may be other specific things that you have to take into consideration.

The kind of care that you want for your horse will be unique to your horse. And having a clear picture will help your discussions with the barn owner. So, with your horse in mind, ask yourself , "what does my horse need in order to be comfortable and healthy?"

Following is a list to help you get started. Add and subtract as you see fit.

— *Basic treatment for cuts and scrapes*

— *Cold hosing in case of a sprained tendon*

— *Fly masks on and off*

— *Fly sheet for the summer months*

— *Application of fly spray*

— *Blanketing when it rains or only when it's really cold. Be specific.*

— *Bandaging*

— *Medication*

— *Supplements that need to be added to his feed*

— *Should be stalled at night and turned out during the day*

— *Can't be left on grass due to laminitis*

— *Can't be turned out on grass due to increased chances of colic*

6. What makes for a fun atmosphere for you?

Trail access, a round pen and an arena is about all I need to have fun. A few barrels and other toys I could use around the arena would be an added bonus. Perhaps a couple of jump standards and I'm in heaven. I'd also like a smaller barn with an adult oriented atmosphere. It'd be great if the others boarders had similar interests as well. Then we could actually do some stuff together. That'd be pretty cool.

You on the other hand may be looking for things to do for your children, or perhaps you're into dressage or jumping and would like to do some shows. If you're into cattle penning you may be looking for a facility that holds cattle for this purpose.

If you have a young horse, you might like to have a trainer on site or at least be allowed to bring your own. What if you wanted to be able to take lessons? Is there an instructor on site, or do you have a favorite you'd like to bring along?

Make a list of the things you'd like to do with your horse. Also write down your own interests and philosophies you hold dear. Do you want an adult oriented barn or would you prefer a family focus? What kind of people or age groups do you want to hang out with? What kind of amenities should the barn have? For example a bathroom, wash stalls, and cross ties. What about the facilities like a round pen, indoor arena, dressage arena, a lounge, etc. Do you need to be able to park your horse trailer at the barn?

7. Make your lists and set your priorities

Now that you have a clear picture of what you'd like to have for yourself and your horse, it's time to set some priorities. It's not only rare to find a place that will be able to accommodate everything, but your available budget will also force you to make some compromises.

So, let's take another look at your lists. But this time identify what you can't live without and what would be nice to have.

And remember, it's much easier for **you** to make a compromise than your horse.

8. Locating and contacting boarding stables...

After I did my bit of "soul searching" I actually felt much better about starting my search. I felt a lot more prepared and ready. I also didn't feel nearly as uncomfortable about picking up the phone and making the initial phone calls. After all, I was clear on my priorities and therefore knew what questions I needed to ask up front and that made a huge difference.

So, Where do You Find these Places that Offer Board for Horses?

Finding places that offer board isn't all that hard. The local tack shops or feed stores often have a bulletin board where boarding stables will post their ads.

You can also check the local magazines. These are often available for free in the tack shops. Don't forget to ask the tack shop keeper if they can make any recommendations. After all they are a central hub for information and talk to tons of people.

The internet is also an excellent place to find out about available board. Some of the local horse organizations may have a web site with a forum where boarding stables are allowed to post their ads. You can also read the posts from other members or ask them if they have any experience with any of the barns in the area, or if there is a place that anyone would recommend. If you're new to the area I think you'll be surprised how willing people are to help out. One thing I have noticed though is that there are not that many boarding stables that actually have a web site, so finding more specific information using the internet could be a little challenging.

Another excellent source of information is your vet or farrier. They travel around a lot and come across a lot of boarding stables and people. Ask them if there are any barns that they would recommend. I would doubt that they would ever tell you to go somewhere that they didn't feel was up to par. Also, don't forget to ask them which barns to avoid. This can save you some unnecessary headaches and wasted time.

Set Up Your Appointments

In order for a barn to make my short list, the ads would have to touch on what I was looking for and the cost of board would of course have to fall within my budget. If I couldn't figure out from the ad whether my needs could be met but it sounded interesting, I would call the barn owner and quickly ask about those things that were high on my list of "must haves". If it still sounds good, I'd find out what time would be best for me to come out and set up an appointment with the barn owner.

That initial conversation with the barn owner will tell you a lot about whether this person is friendly and easy to talk to and whether you may like this person. That's provided you get to talk to a person!

A friend of mine had a crazy experience that left us both kind of baffled. She was going on vacation with her horse and looking for a temporary home for him close to where she'd be. She called this place but had to leave a message. Half an hour later she received a call back, but instead of it being a live person, it was a recorded message with a whole bunch of instructions from this barn.

She was appalled and I had to agree. It was so impersonal to the point of being rude. Why would you want to put your horse in the care of someone who can't even be bothered to talk to you in person??

First impressions are very important, though you can't base everything on just that. Sometimes you get a person on the wrong day. If the rest sounds good, give it a second chance and see if your first impression still stands.

Go for Your Drive

Bring a friend. It's much easier to take in all the details when you have a buddy system going. You can talk to the barn owner and ask your questions, while your friend observes and makes note of the general condition of things.

It's also a good idea to bring a digital camera. It will help you remember the different places. Depending on how many you have on your list, by the end of the day it gets hard to keep them all apart.

When you go for your drive to visit the different barns on your list, make a note of the day and time of day. What is the weather like? How far is it? How busy is the traffic? How long does it take to get to the barn? This is especially important if you have to consider your work schedule and risk battling rush hour traffic.

PART TWO
Visiting the Facilities

HOW TO FIND TROUBLE FREE HORSE BOARDING

CHAPTER 2
The Business Side of Things

I'm thankful that I understand what it takes to run a business. That doesn't mean there is no room for improvement, but at least I do have a solid background to draw from.

When I started my journey it certainly was a leap of faith. I had no idea what I was getting myself into. My world unfolded in front of me and I just kept on making the next step. I have heard of others having similar stories – we just love horses, so why not?

There are many aspects to running a boarding stable and it's not for the faint of heart. It's not only about taking care of the horses, making sure their needs are met and that they are fed and watered. It also means planning and ordering supplies; managing employees; scheduling appointments with farriers and vets; arranging for materials, labor, and making repairs; and budgeting for major expenses and improvements.

You also have to keep owners abreast of anything that goes on with their horses; screening new applicants and making sure new horses meet the health requirements. New boarders coming in should mix well with the current group. After all it's the barn owner's responsibility to build a community but it also should be a place where they enjoy going to work.

Once new horses come to live at the facility, the transition and integration of the new horse need to be carefully monitored. This is a stressfull time not only for the new horse, but also the owner, the horses already living at the barn, other boarders and the barn owner. It takes time for new routines to set in and for everything to find a new happy balance.

I think one of the biggest challenges we face as barn owners in this business is the difference between the cost of running a place like this properly and what people are prepared and able to pay. The cost of living goes up much faster than salary increases gobbling up our disposable income at rapid rates.

Barns are hit almost weekly with price increases on feed, lumber, and bedding for example. This year alone with the rise in gas prices and fertilizer we're going to be in for some unpleasant surprises. For some keeping a horse is not going to be a possibility anymore.

A second challenge we face is the lack of understanding and recognition of what it takes to run a facility like this. The amount of work and time commitment is phenomenal. Horses are hard on their environment and surroundings need to be maintained regularly. People can be quite demanding of the needs for their horses, reasonable or not, and then get upset if board prices are being raised or they get an extra bill. Some simply don't pay their board.

I have seen a number of barn owners get into this business with great enthusiasm and big plans only to find them a year later disillusioned and no longer willing to go the extra distance.

1. The barn owner or manager...
How can you tell that they know their stuff?

I have certainly learned that running a boarding stable is multi faceted and requires a lot of knowledge and skill. Something a lot of people underestimate. And it's not just dealing with the horses – what about all the boarders? They all have their wishes and believes of what is right and what is not. The more boarders and horses, the more complex everything gets. You need more than just someone who is good with horses and their care. You also need someone who is a real people person and who understands business.

Trusting the well being of my horse to a stranger isn't something I do easily. If there are things I'm not happy about, or things I want adjusted or monitored, or just have a few questions, I want to be able to talk to the barn owner and not feel like I'm a major inconvenience to them.

Apart from me liking them I also need to feel comfortable that they know how to assess a horse's well being and know what to do in the case of an emergency.

And what about general nutrition, handling and integrating horses in to new herds, or help settling a horse in to his new home? Do they understand the risks and do they know how to monitor the horse?

So how do you know you have a person that knows their stuff, is personable, trustworthy, responsible, and knows how to run the business aspects? Do they keep their promises? Do they make feed changes without much forethought? Are they on top of the repairs? Do they make improvements to the facility?

A lot of these questions could perhaps be best answered by the other boarders and it's a good idea to talk to them, especially the ones that have been there for a while. Make note whether you feel comfortable with the other boarders. Do they say *Hi* and greet you? Do they seem on good terms with the barn owner?

If you want to get a feel whether or not the barn owner is responsible and takes her work seriously, take a good look around – does the facility look clean and well organized or are things kind of chaotic with stuff lying all over the place? This is usually a good reflection of the barn owner, but also of the boarders who board there.

I'd like to share a little story here about the "broken window" theory ... If a place is in disarray – binder twine lying around, garbage overflowing, tack boxes with stuff stacked on top of them, brushes everywhere, the broken stall door, the leaking waterer ... these would all be considered "broken windows". The "broken windows" invite more "broken windows". People using or visiting the place will have less respect for their surroundings and will add to the disorder instead of trying to clean up or keep it clean. Why would they... nobody cares anyway, right? On the flip side, if a place is clean and organized, those using the facility are less likely to go out of bounds and instead keep it orderly and clean as well.

Questions to Ask...

— *How much experience do they have with horses?*

— *How long have they been involved and what is their background?*

— *Do they have any professional training?*

— *How long have they been running a boarding establishment?*

— *Can they give you any references?*

— *Do they handle the horses themselves or do they have staff handling the horses?*

- *Is staff supervised?*
- *Are horses matched with appropriate handlers?*
- *Does the barn owner live on site? If not, how are the horses monitored?*
- *Does the barn owner have another day job off site?*
- *If you were out of town, would they be keeping in touch with you?*
- *Are they technologically savvy?*
- *Could they send digital photos in case there was an emergency?*

Things to Observe ...

- *What is your first impression of this person?*
- *Does this person come across as mature and responsible?*
- *How are they answering your questions? Do you get the feeling that they're knowledgeable but also willing to work with you?*
- *Is this a person you can talk to easily?*
- *Are they courteous and quick to get back to you?*
- *Do you feel you could learn from them?*
- *Based on the information they provide, do you get the feeling that they're honest and knowledgeable?*
- *Watch how the barn owner interacts with other boarders and staff. Does it look like there is a good relationship or do things appear strained?*
- *Does the barn owner do what he/she says they're going to do or are there a lot of empty promises? This is a good question to ask other boarders who have already been there for a little while.*

2. What is the cost of board and what is included? Are you making assumptions?

When I was new to boarding, and new to horse ownership, I didn't know to pay attention to things like blanketing, type of feed, fly masks on and off. Actually, I paid attention to it, but was pretty clueless when it came to knowing what to look for or what were reasonable expectations to have. Wasn't that automatically part of the package anyway and the boarding facility's responsibility?

You know what – it isn't. It's like the old adage "buyer beware".

I do need to share a story with you though... I have come across stables that have separate charges for just about everything. When I was looking at a pricing structure for my boarding stable, I initially thought it was perhaps a good idea since some horses are such easy keepers and others are not.

Then one day a friend of mine came to me for help to get her horses moved. Where she boarded, boarders were charged for every single blanket change, fly mask on and off, bandaging, basic medical attention, turn in/turn out, etc. The problem was that for each service provided they would need the okay from the owner since it would incur a charge.

One of her horses ended up with an ugly cut and was put in a stall while having her fly mask on. She was just left like that until the barn finally contacted my friend. After all, it would cost her extra money to have the fly mask taken off and the horse looked at. The question that immediately came to my mind was "how long did it take for the barn to make contact with the owner and how long was this horse left unattended?"

What I learned from this is that by having separate charges for everything, a boarding stable paralyzes itself and therefore compromises the well being of your horse. Not cool.

My solution has been to provide a few different packages so that boarders can choose which they believe to be better suited for their horse. Plus, it puts me in a position where I can simply do what's right for the horse, especially when I can't get a hold of the owner.

So, full board, but also self and semi board, have many different definitions and what is included varies from stable to stable. You really need to be aware of where the boundaries lie because not only your available budget will be affected but more importantly your horse ends up taking the brunt of it all. And that's exactly what we're trying to avoid.

Another note of caution here: **DO NOT go for the cheapest price!** The extra charges may well put you over budget.

Secondly, a horse with an injury due to improper care or unsafe surroundings can become more costly than paying a higher price for board where you know your horse is safe and properly looked after.

Also, **don't settle for a place that's too expensive for you** regardless of how much you like it. It catches up with you in a hurry forcing you to move again to something more affordable. This is really not fair to your horse. Moving is very hard on them.

Lastly, property maintenance is expensive. I know board will seem expensive to you, but if the facility doesn't charge enough they won't be able to keep up with the repairs and ensure a safe place. We'll be covering more on this when we look at the different things to look for in and around the barn.

A quick note about extra charges for feed and bedding … as a boarder I was always of the mindset that these should simply be part of the board regardless of how much the horse uses. In fact, I never knew what my horse really needed when I boarded him.

But the reality is that all horses are individuals. Some get fat just looking at food whereas others just burn calories breathing. If you have a hard keeper you have to expect extra charges for feed, and quite frankly, I would want to see the extra charges because at least I'll know that my horse is fed what it needs and that the facility won't be skimping to save costs.

Bedding is another one that could incur extra charges. Some horses simply are pigs and go through bedding like there is no tomorrow, especially youngsters; or perhaps you'd like your horse's bedding to be nice and deep. Bedding is very expensive and the boarding stable has to stay on budget, so if you want more than what is budgeted for, expect to pay the difference. And it's not only about the cost of bedding … more bedding also means more waste and bigger manure piles that must be managed or hauled away.

Questions to Ask…

— *Is there more than one boarding option to choose from?*

— *What are the costs?*

— *What exactly is included?*

— *Is deworming included with board?*

— *Does the option offered suit my needs?*

— *Is there room for customization? How much more will it cost?*

— *What is the hourly barn rate?*

— *Is all feed and bedding included or could I be subject to extra charges?*

— *Is there a feed and/or bedding budget per horse?*

— *Board increases, how often do these take place?*

— *Are there any extra charges for blanketing, fly masks on/off, basic medical care or bandaging?*

3. The application process and contract... If these are absent, how will you know that business is taken seriously?

During my boarding days I never came across a barn that required me to fill out an application form let alone sign a contract or required me to have proof of vaccines or perform specific tests on my horse.

That always left me with some uneasy feelings though. What about the next boarder and horse coming in? Would we get along? Would they be disruptive to the current environment that I enjoy so much right now? Would the new horse be aggressive or bring in disease? Where is this new horse going to be living? And come to think of it, I'm not really sure what criteria the barn owner has for accepting new boarders and horses. Hmmm.

I'm sure some of these questions have been in the back of your mind as well when you hear that a new boarder is about to join the group.

When I started my boarding stable I was warned by trainers and other ex-barn managers to make sure I did my due diligence before accepting people to stay at my place. I took that to heart and am glad I did, though it wasn't an easy journey.

The first person I attracted was highly offended by the process which didn't leave me feeling too good. However, what I learned is that those that are willing to go through the application process really want to be here and are good, solid people.

In fact my boarders love to make fun of my screening process: "That was worse and more nerve racking than my final math exam!" they'll say. Though in the same breath they'll tell me how nice and considerate everyone is at the barn and how much they appreciate me taking the time to make sure we have the right mix.

I think a proper application and screening process is an absolute must. For one you'll know that everyone who boards at this place has gone through the same screening process. It also shows pride and self respect from the barn owner.

Not only do they make sure that their business can survive, but they're also taking responsibility for building a community that is safe and fun for both you and your horse. In fact the questions on the application should give you a good idea of what's important to the barn owner.

Here are some things that you could expect to see on an application form:

- Personal references and previous boarding history
- Questions about what you like to do with your horse
- Questions about your horse's general health and any medical requirements
- Vaccines and deworming
- Vet and farrier information

When you are given the application form ask the barn owner for a copy of the contract and barn rules as well. This will give you some time to think it through and you'll get a good idea of what the expectations are. If there are things you're unclear about, just ask for clarification. A quick email or phone call should be enough. This will also give you another opportunity to see whether you get along with the barn owner.

The contract will outline the expectations and responsibilities of both you and the boarding stable. If there are disputes then this becomes your starting point.

What are some of the things you could expect to see in a contract?

- Information about your horse
- Proof of ownership
- Fees and terms
- Emergency care
- Stable rules
- Notice of termination
- Special instructions to the stable
- Liability waiver

Questions to Ask...

— *What is their selection criterion for new boarders?*

— *Is there a particular philosophy or discipline that they prefer to focus on?*

— *What is the criterion for their horses that they will accept into the facility? Certain breeds, temperament, age, sex, performance or retired?*

— *Does the barn owner actually take the time to meet the new horse as part of the screening process?*

— *Are there any required vaccines that the horses must have before coming on the property?*

— *Is a Coggins test required? Any other tests?*

— *How quickly will they make their decision?*

— *What is the maximum number of boarders or boarded horses the facility will accept?*

— *Can you have a copy of the boarding contract and barn rules?*

— *Is there an emergency contact form included with the contract?*

4. The transition process for you and your horse... Is this stressful time handled properly?

Since I have to entrust my dearest friend to total strangers and a new environment, I don't take the decision of moving my boy lightly.

In one respect it's an exciting time because I think the change is a positive one for both of us. However, in the same breath it certainly puts me on edge because I sure hope I've made the right decision and, most of all, that I haven't overlooked anything!

Making a move go as smoothly as possible is very important since a horse that's under great stress may not drink for example and could end up with colic as a result of impaction.

So, to make sure that the entire move goes well you need the barn owner on your side. A good barn owner knows what works and hasn't worked in the past with other horses and what to watch for. They also know who would make a good fence buddy to help settle your horse.

But…

They also need **your** knowledge about your horse to help them understand particular stress reactions that your horse may display. They have to monitor your horse when you're not there to make sure he's ok. Water intake for example is extremely important. Remember, they don't know your horse intimately like you do, at least not at this stage. Team work is definitely key here.

Of course, you may have just purchased your horse and don't really know either. In that case you're really relying on the experience of the barn owner. But one thing you can do to help is solicit as much information as possible from the previous owner. This can really help the process.

Ask the barn owner how they will help your horse settle in. Will they make time for you and your horse on the day you arrive? If you felt so inclined, would they even let you curl up on a cot in the stall with him for the night?

Yes, that has happened to me, and it certainly was a first for me. My biggest concern was the safety of my new boarder, but I did let her try it out on a per night basis. It was a stretch for me because apart from her safety I was also concerned about the liability issues in case things went wrong, but hey, if it works and nobody gets hurt, why not?

From the barn owner's perspective, here are a couple of things that have worked well for me.

I like the horse to arrive at a time when all the cleaning and feeding are finished. Usually late morning, but this is something unique to every barn. With the peace returned in the barn the new arrival can move into a quiet space.

And with my distractions gone I can spend some quality time with the new horse and owner. It also gives your horse the chance to take in the new surroundings, smells and sounds while it's daylight.

I prefer to put the horse in a paddock rather than straight into a field. For some horses a large space just becomes too overwhelming so I choose to start small and work my way out as they get more comfortable.

I'll watch him for a while with the owner and find a quiet fence buddy. Once the horse has quieted down, we may take him for a walk around the property and introduce him to some of the horses and surroundings. From there on it's really the horse that tells me what step is next.

If the transition is difficult I keep a daily diary and watch their water and feed intake and elimination and stay in close contact with the owner to make sure I'm not missing any signs. If the transition is easy then we can start looking at finding him some compatible friends.

This works in my environment. You need to find out from the barn owner what they will do and how they will help you and your horse with the transition.

Questions to Ask...

— *How many new horses will they accept at the same time? The more horses they take in at once, the more divided their attention will be.*

— *Is there a preferred time they'd like you to arrive? Do they care?*

— *Are they taking their busy times into consideration? Arriving during busy times can be unsettling for new horses coming in.*

— *How will the stall and/or paddock be prepared for your horse? For example, do they disinfect the stall before you arrive, does your horse get a new salt block, is the waterer completely cleaned out? Do they get new bedding?*

— *Will the barn owner make some time for you to help your horse settle in, show you around and introduce you to any of the boarders if they're around?*

— *How would the horse be monitored if they're having a difficult time adjusting?*

— *What about feed changes or are they okay to feed your horse his regular fair for the first little while until he has settled in?*

— *In case you can't be there with your horse and your horse has difficulty adjusting, how will you be kept abreast of your horse's progress? Are they willing to give you daily reports until he has settled down?*

5. Daily handling of your horse... Is your horse in good hands?

When trusting my horse to strangers, I'm always worried about how he's being handled and concerned that he may end up with emotional issues or become disrespectful due to poor horsemanship skills or practices.

I love my horse and would never think to abuse him. I treat my horse with kindness, understanding and respect while being clear on appropriate behavior and setting fair boundaries for him. I know I expect the boarding stable to handle him in much the same manner as I do and I'm sure you feel the same.

But considering the number of different philosophies on what is appropriate around horses it's only fair that we are very clear on how we want our horse to be handled, what we'll accept and won't accept and then choose the boarding stable accordingly.

Since I follow the principles of natural horsemanship, my best solution is to find a barn where they follow the same philosophy.

That way I have a good chance that my horse has the consistency he needs and I don't end up correcting my horse to undo what was done in the handling during my absence.

When I have to start correcting him I really feel like I've let my best friend down and that I may need to look for another place again.

◀ *Ritter and his handler*

Because really, it's not fair to him when one person says "yes" and the other says "no" to the same thing. Wouldn't you agree?

Now, there shouldn't be a huge amount of interaction between the staff and your horse at the barn. However there are some daily practices that you will want to see and some that you really do not want.

For instance, a handler's skill level should be matched appropriately with the horses they are responsible for. The more experienced handlers should be managing the more demanding horses.

Horses should also be led into their stalls, paddocks, or pastures. I have heard of cases where all the gates just get opened up and it's a free for all. This is very dangerous, not to mention that the horse may well lose all respect for people and little by little can turn into an absolute menace.

In fact I was working with an ex-stallion where evening turn in was exactly like this and it was the barn's daily practice. After only a month of him being at that facility he was completely out of hand and downright dangerous.

The daily handling reinforces who's the leader (which should be the human!), appropriate behavior and boundaries which are all equally important.

I certainly don't have a problem if two horses, or even three for that matter, are led at the same time provided they're well matched and the handler has the appropriate skill level. But as soon as any one of the horses display any sign of disrespect they should be led one-by-one until things settle back to proper respectful behavior.

Handling isn't only an issue in full-board facilities. When you do self- or semi-board, you typically end up sharing the duties with other boarders. One person may take care of the morning feed and turn out, another takes care of the evening, a third could be doing the weekend together with a fourth. That's a lot of people handling your horse!

And where are they at with their horse handling skills? Do they share the same philosophies as you? If you didn't like these people handling your horse, would you be able to take care of your horse seven days per week, morning and night?

Questions to Ask...

— *Who handles the horses and are the handlers supervised?*

— *What seems to be the average age of the handlers?*

— *Is the temperament of a horse matched to the skill level of the handler?*

— *Does the barn have minimum skill requirements for those who work there? Will they train their staff?*

— *Do they show concern for the safety of their staff? Personally I like to visit the horses before they come onto my property so that I know who will need to manage the horse for example.*

— *Do they have a baseline for what they consider a "well mannered and safe horse"?*

— *Do the horses get led to their pastures, paddocks and stalls?*

— *Are horses treated as individuals and according to their personalities or are they just a number?*

Things to Observe ...

— *Do you see handlers or other boarders treat their horses roughly?*

— *Are the horses treated with kindness?*

— *How is the barn owner around the horses?*

— *How do the horses respond to the barn owner? Are they respectful or pushy?*

— *Do the horses approach the handlers or do they walk away?*

6. Health care requirements...
Herd health is essential! But is taken seriously?

The thing that worries me the most is that my horse may pick up some kind of illness from another horse that just came in to the barn. One of the most commonly feared diseases is Equine Infectious Anemia (EIA) and can be detected with a Coggins test. Horses coming from areas where EIA is common should be required to have a Coggin's test before being allowed to stay at the barn.

Strangles is another highly contagious and serious infection. Horses can be carriers and you'd never know that they were infected. There is apparently a blood test that could be performed to see if a horse is a carrier. I'm actually checking into this with my vet as we speak. A test like this could be performed before horses are allowed to stay in the barn.

A boarding stable should have proper vaccination requirements and health checks to prevent these kinds of diseases from entering the barn. If the barn doesn't adopt a solid health care policy I would not be comfortable putting my horse there. And don't let yourself get sent astray with comments like "horses rarely ever come and go here, so we don't worry about it". It only takes a visit to a clinic or show to pick up something.

On a few occasions I've come across barns where suddenly there is an outbreak of Strangles only to hear later that it was a new arrival who was the carrier. They rarely had horses coming and going – it only takes one.

In all honesty – though I firmly believe vaccination has to be a requirement – I do question the fact that they should be done every 6 months or year. There is enough data out there that suggests that we're over vaccinating and doing more harm than good.

There is a titre test that can be done to determine whether the horse still has enough immunity to certain diseases. These tests tend to be more expensive than the vaccines though. But if the frequency of vaccines is a big concern for you, ask the boarding stable whether they'd be ok with you going the alternate route. Check first with your vet though to see whether he can do the titre tests for you.

A regular deworming schedule is another very important component of health care and everyone at the barn should adhere to it otherwise you're just throwing your money away. I think it's best if the deworming is included with the board and that the barn takes responsibility for it. That way, you know everyone is done and is on the same schedule.

Why should everyone be on the same schedule you ask? Worms have a lifecycle and deworming all the horses at the same time prevents an increase in larvae population. You can learn more about this by researching deworming practices on the internet. It's quite an in-depth subject and outside the scope of this book.

When I had my first horse I was quite naïve about some of these things and just simply didn't do them. Was I supposed to? I know, it sounds silly, but yes, I too was new to horse ownership at one point in my life. When a boarding stable takes the responsibility for this, you won't have to worry about others not doing their part.

Hoof care needs to be done regularly as well and a well managed barn will make sure that all horses, and not just their own, are monitored even if boarders take care of their own appointments.

Horse's teeth should be regularly floated by either a vet or equine dentist. Some barns may require this as part of the yearly health requirements; others just leave it up to the owners.

If the teeth have hooks and are uneven, it's difficult for the horse to properly eat and grind their feed. When the horse can't grind its feed properly it also can't get the proper nutrition from it and much of the food ends up getting wasted. A barn owner should let you know when they think the teeth should be checked since they see the changes in the way your horse eats.

Questions to Ask...

— *What are the required vaccines for all the horses on the property?*

— *Do they require horses to have a Coggins test done before coming to stay at the facility?*

— *Do they have any testing requirements in place for Strangles?*

— *Would they be open to titre tests?*

— *Is deworming done by the barn or is this left up to the boarders? Is everyone on the same schedule?*

— *If deworming is done by the boarders, does the barn keep track of when everyone is done? How do they monitor this?*

— *Does the barn have any involvement with vaccines, deworming, hoof care or other health care requirements?*

— *Does the barn require their boarders to do annual dental exams?*

Things to Observe ...

— *Do the horses appear curious and interested or are they dull and bored looking?*

— *Do coats look shiny and are feet well trimmed and taken care off?*

— *Do paddocks look clean or do they have weeks of built up manure? What about the pastures?*

7. Vet, farrier, and other health care professionals... Who's on board?

If you're like me, then you're probably quite particular about who looks after your horse's feet and medical care. One of the first things that I will ask is who the barn uses for their vet and farriery services, and whether they'd have an issue with me bringing my own. It is possible that the barn may have issues with certain vets or farriers so make sure you ask.

There are some definite advantages to using the barn vet. Farm calls can get expensive and for simple routine care like vaccines and dentistry, it's more efficient to get into the pool and be able to share the call fee with other boarders.

If the barn arranges for these kinds of things you'll know that they're on top of things and that there is a good chance that everyone is up to date. If everything is left up to the boarders and

▼ *"Who are we trimming today?"*

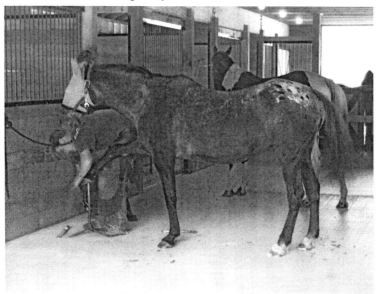

without a proper monitoring plan in place by the stable, I'd be quite concerned and not comfortable at all with boarding my horse there.

The downside can be that these calls are arranged at times when it's convenient for the barn and not for you so you'll need to decide how important it is for you to be there.

You'll also want to check whether there will be extra charges to stand for the vet or farrier, and if so, at what rate.

The barn is likely to have a good rapport with their vet and farrier which can work in your favor. In the case of an emergency, they may give it a higher priority because of the business relationship they have. Sometimes the barn may be able to arrange for some bulk deals and pass on the savings to the boarders. And if you don't have a vet or farrier yet you can take advantage of an already established relationship.

▼ *If you don't already have a health care professional, you can take advantage of the relationships that the barn already has in place.*

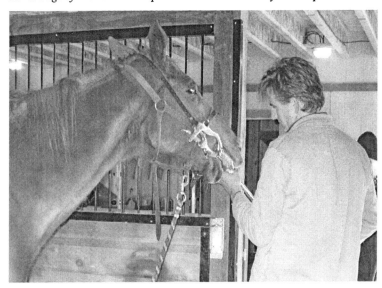

If you prefer to use your own vet and farrier, then you should expect to arrange your own appointments and take care of your horse during these times. In some cases the barn may agree to make the arrangements with your specified vet or farrier for you, so it's worth asking. Do check whether there may be extra charges for this though.

Questions to Ask...

— *Which vet currently visits the barn?*

— *Which farrier currently visits the barn?*

— *How long have the vet and farrier served the barn or worked with the barn owner?*

— *Do they have an alternate in case their regular guys are unavailable?*

— *Does the barn organize farrier or vet visits or are these the responsibility of the owner?*

— *Can you bring your own vet and farrier?*

— *Check with your own vet and farrier whether they will come to the barn you're thinking off choosing.*

— *Will the barn arrange for routine visits to cut down on farm calls and help boarders save on fees?*

— *Is the vet trained in equine dentistry or is there a separate equine dentist that comes to the barn?*

— *Are there any vets, farriers or other health care professionals that are not welcome at the barn? Why not?*

— *What other health care professionals like acupuncture, massage, chiropractors, holistic practitioners, etc. come to the barn?*

8. Storage of feed, supplements & medication... Proper storage is a necessity!

The places where I stayed typically had the feed and tack in the same place. I didn't think it was ideal, particularly when the tack room was small. There was always a lot of dust, especially if the space had a concrete floor, plus it was hard to keep things neat and tidy.

Open bags or spilled feed also contributed to rodent problems and, let me tell you, those rodents just loved my saddle pads and cleaning rags! And let's not forget those few times my heart skipped a few beats when one jumped out of my tack box!

Yah, I know they're cute …

SO!!?

In one place all the grain was stored in an old freezer - I mean all the feed bags were simply dumped in there and then at feeding time each horse would get a scoop. I always wondered about how old the feed would be and if there was any mold. In hind sight I realize too that there was no consideration when it came to the individual needs of the horses.

And what about supplements and medication? These can be expensive. If a feed room is publicly accessible, there is no guarantee that someone else will not help themselves. And lastly one of my biggest fears is to find my horse rummaging around in the feed room, helping himself to all the tasty treats and working himself up to a nasty colic and expensive vet bill, not to mention death.

Even if the feed is stored in animal proof bins a horse will still find ways to get into it. A feed room that is publicly accessible is bound to have the door left open from time to time so this is a serious consideration in my books.

As I'm sure you've already guessed, my vote definitely goes toward a separate and secure feed room accessible only to authorized staff whenever possible. However, this setup works for full board only.

With self and semi board you'll come across a variety of arrangements. What I have found in my journey is that few places are set up properly. I've seen a couple of semi-board stables where they had a storage area either in or near the stall that you could call your own and lock up. In other cases it was a small room shared by a few boarders or a large hay loft with a bunch of "personal" piles. Be extra aware of how things are kept and secured while keeping in mind the things I've mentioned earlier.

Questions to Ask...

— *Where is additional feed stored? Mice and rats could be a consideration.*

— *Do they keep health records and emergency contact information on the horses? Where are these kept?*

— *If you'd like to have supplements added to your horse's feed, is there a safe place where these can be stored?*

— *Is there a charge to have these added to your horse's feed?*

— *Does the barn carry a number of supplements, and if so, would they let you purchase them from the barn? Would they charge you the current market rates?*

— *Can you bring your own feed? Is there enough room to store it? Are they willing to bring it in? If not, will what they provide give your horse the nutrition he needs?*

Things to Observe ...

— *Is there a separate feed room or is it part of the tack room?*

— *Is the feed room publicly accessible or is it secure and only accessible to staff?*

— *Is the feed room clean and organized?*

— *Is the feed stored in animal proof bins?*

— *Is there a sink and hot water? This helps keeping buckets and utensils clean but also for preparing feed and beet pulp. The vet will appreciate having access to hot water too.*

— *How clean is the floor? Feed on the floor will attract mice and rats.*

— *What is the floor made of? Concrete attracts dust; tile can get slippery but is much easier to keep clean.*

— *Do you see weigh scales and weigh tapes hanging anywhere?*

— *Is there a fridge to keep medication or other things cool?*

— *If the barn keeps supplements, make a note of what they seem to favor.*

— *If there are supplements from other boarders, are they labeled with the boarder's name?*

— *Is there a first aid kit anywhere? Do you see any sprays or ointments for cuts and scrapes?*

— *Do they keep a white or black board in the feed room for quick notes? If yes, you might want to take a quick peek to see what is written on it. It may give some other insight.*

— *Any signs of rats and/or mice? Look for bait stations or any other type of pest control. A cat counts too!*

9. Feed and feed changes...
Are meals planned and changes made with forethought?

The horse's gut is very sensitive and sudden changes can cause some unpleasant surprises. Moving your horse is stressful for him and may very well upset his gut, so it's a good idea to introduce change in stages.

I find it is best not to introduce feed changes until he has settled in. Once he's relaxed and settled with his environment – and how long this takes is different for every horse – you can start to change his feed – GRADUALLY!

And as a rule of thumb for **any** feed changes, changes should **always** be made gradually. Be aware that some barns run on such a tight budget that they will buy only the cheapest feeds or that what

◀ *I love the feed room in my barn. It's separate, secure, organized, and easy to keep clean.*

is on special without ever thinking about this. Consistency in feed is very important for a horse.

Horses are herbivores and designed to eat grass. At least 80% of their diet should consist of hay, grass or a combination. Grain should come into consideration when you need to make up a calorie short fall or wish to use it as an agent for supplements. If you'd like to learn more about nutrition there are some excellent books you can read. You can find some of these on my web site as well at **HorseBoardingSecrets.com**

The main thing is that your horse gets the necessary nutrients so that he's healthy and can perform at the levels you require of him. This can be accomplished with a variety of feeds and supplements; it just takes a little forethought. The big question is though: how will you be able to tell whether or not the chosen feeds are in fact beneficial to your horse?

A horse needs fiber in his gut, and lots of it. Be careful with pelletized feeds since some have a tendency to absorb a lot of water. Remember what they tell you about Beet Pulp? You have to add at least 4 cups of water to 1 cup of Beet Pulp otherwise your horse may colic due to an impaction because of the expansion rate and volume. Well, some of these pelletized feeds are no better! Don't believe me? Go ahead, and play with it! I have and I was shocked with some of the results.

So, how do you know whether horses are being fed enough forage?

I like to take a walk through the paddocks or stalls and look at the consistency of the manure. There should be evidence of a lot of fiber. Stool shouldn't be all clumped together like a solid pasty pile either. You want to see nicely formed "apples".

Of course no horse is the same, but when things are kind of pasty and compacted and there is hardly any visible fiber, I will start quizzing the barn manager about what they're feeding and why and what is the situation with THAT particular horse.

Do you see big, spread out patties? The birds may be playing a factor here! This is especially true in spring time, so don't confuse these with diarrhea. I know they had me puzzled for a while! And you thought your job was easy.

Questions to Ask...

— *What kind of experience do they have with the nutritional requirements of horses? Any official training or a genuine personal interest?*

— *What is their rational behind their feeding program?*

— *What is the hay to grain ratio fed to the horses?*

— *How will they switch the horse from his current diet to a new diet? Is it done gradually?*

— *If major changes are required in the future, will you be included in the process?*

— *What kind of hay types are being fed and why?*

— *Do they feed grass and alfalfa separately or is the hay a grass/ alfalfa mix?*

— *What if your horse can't have alfalfa, is that a problem or do they brush it off that a little alfalfa can't hurt?*

— *Where does the hay come from? Will they let you have a look at the hay?*

— *Do they ever run out of hay?*

— *If your horse has special needs like scheduled medication, can the barn in fact accommodate these? Mornings and evenings will be easier to accommodate than mid-day and night time.*

Things to Observe ...

— *Do the horses look well fed or skinny? Do they have a shiny coat or is it dull?*

— *Do the horses have good looking feet or are they cracked and broken up?*

— *Does the manure look nicely formed and fibrous? You should be able to see the digested hay easily in the stool.*

— *Is the hay nice and green? Does it have a good smell or does it smell moldy? Is there any dust?*

— *Does the hay storage look neat and tidy?*

— *Do they ask you what your horse is currently fed?*

— *Do they show you around the feed room and show you what they carry and explain why?*

10. Feeding routines...
What is really going on?

When I looked around for board, I would see ads that would advertise 2 feedings, 3 feedings, or even 5 or 6 feedings per day. When I actually started to talk to some of these places I would find out that 5 or 6 feedings would count the grain as a single feeding regardless whether it was fed at the same time as the hay or not. So, 5 feedings were really 3.

I have often asked myself whether it was better to have my horse fed 2 or 3 times per day or just free choice. As a barn owner I've tried several approaches and what I've learned is that there really is no set answer. Every horse is different but it also depends on the living environment of the horse – do they have access to pasture, paddock or no turn out for example.

Each horse needs a certain amount of calories per day and it varies from horse to horse. The older horses tend to eat much slower and will take all day to finish their morning hay.

On the other end of the spectrum I have had one horse that could live on air, vacuums his hay in 45 minutes flat putting Hoover to shame and who would eat as many bales you'd give him – he's obsessed with food.

I tried splitting his morning hay into breakfast and lunch so it would last longer. I ended up with a very unhappy and miserable horse. I had to go back to two feedings a day with him and just let him roam and pick his way through the pasture for the rest of the time. He's a much happier boy for it.

With the smaller portions he never reached a satiation point and was always hungry. If you feed good quality hay, you have to portion things based on the horse's individual calorie requirements. Some horses will simply eat way more than what they need and put on weight like crazy which only leads to trouble. For that reason and the cost of hay, free choice isn't an option for me.

This system works for me, but if your horse is stabled or is turned out in a paddock for the day, the picture changes. These horses don't have any opportunity to be a horse and pick at things all day long. A horse is designed to be eating and moving constantly, so to keep the gut functions safe and to combat boredom, feeding more often becomes important. So when discussing feeding frequencies, keep in mind how your horse would be living at that barn.

We're such creatures of habit that it's easy to get in the groove of feeding at set times; however, it's a good idea to be a bit more flexible about the whole thing. A flexible feeding schedule teaches them not to anticipate and get all worked up because the barn owner didn't arrive at 5pm because they happen to get stuck in traffic. Stuff happens.

For me a 1-2 hour feeding window morning and evening works well. It creates a much quieter and happy group of horses. They don't panic when that flake of hay arrives an hour later. They know that it will get there. And just because I showed my face, doesn't mean the grain buckets are prepared immediately either.

I like to mix things up and be unpredictable. For me there is nothing more stressful than having a row of horses banging on their stall doors because they want their food – NOW! It always reminds me of one of those prison scenes where everyone is banging on the table with their forks. Don't ask me why that picture comes to mind, it just does.

When looking around the barn, ask the barn owner when they typically feed all the horses. How many feedings per day do they do, and if the horse gets grain when will that usually be? Do all the horses get the same food or do they make adjustments for the individuals?

Where are the horses fed? In the pasture, stall, or paddock? Take a look at these areas, and if horses are eating, go check it out. Do you like what you see? Where and how do they get their grain? Is it put in a bucket that has been secured but can easily be removed and cleaned or is it thrown on the dirt or mud? What kinds of buckets are being used? Are they removable or are they permanent plastic or wooden boxes where the grain just gets dumped in?

Do you see any signs of rat droppings? I've had one person, who was looking for a new place for her horse, come to the barn telling me that where she was currently boarded, the rats were eating with her horse out of the same bucket! That's a little too cozy for me.

Now, rodents are pretty well a given around a barn, but things like bait stations, cats, and keeping food supplies sealed up and floors clean make a huge difference in keeping the rodent population at bay.

When hay is fed will the barn take the herd dynamics into consideration or just spread the hay in places that are convenient to them with little consideration for the horses? When feeding horses in a group for example, it's usually a good idea to have more piles than there are horses. That way everyone gets to eat.

Personally, I like to look at the herd dynamics and feed accordingly. For example I have a group of mares that are excellent in sharing so I tend to give them their portions close together. My group of geldings on the other hand, loves to play musical hay and push and shove each other off the piles. So in their case I will make multiple piles with a reasonable distance between them.

Does the stable keep an eye on the least dominant horse, making sure it's getting its fair share of food and doesn't lose weight? What will they do if they find that this horse is not getting enough? Will they put that horse with another horse or in a different herd and see if that works better? Or will they separate the horse so it can eat by itself?

See what kind of answers the barn owner will give you. These should give you a good indication whether this person understands horses and their dynamics. But the answers will also tell you whether the barn owner is willing to work with the dynamics or would rather ignore them.

I know... lots to think about hey?

Questions to Ask ...

— *How often is new feed brought in?*

— *Have they ever run out of feed or hay?*

— *When are the horses typically being fed?*

— *How many feedings per day does the barn do?*

— *If the horse gets grain, when will that usually be given to him?*

— *Is every horse fed the same or do they have a customized feeding program that takes the individual's needs into consideration?*

— *What are the horses typically being fed?*

— *Where are the horses typically being fed? In the pasture, paddock or stall? Or a combination? I often feed hay in the field and grain in the stall for example.*

— *If buckets are used to feed grain, how often are they cleaned out?*

— *How is hay being distributed in group situations?*

— *How do they compensate for the least dominant horse? Do they keep an eye on its weight and make sure it gets his necessary share of the food?*

— *What if a horse starts to drop weight? What will they do?*

— *Will they bring in special hay if your horse cannot eat the regular fair? Don't get upset if the stable says "no". A stable has multiple horses to consider so those coming to stay at the barn have to fit within their system. Hay is typically bought in bulk so for them to bring in special hay for one horse is not always economical.*

— *Will they wet or soak the hay if your horse has a respiratory problem? If so, is there an extra charge for this?*

Things to Observe ...

— *Check out the areas where horses are being fed – pasture, paddock and stall; are they clean and safe?*

— *If the horses are eating, do you like what you see? Are horses fed in piles a distance apart; or are they fed in a great big pile and everyone is to fend for themselves?*

— *Do the horses look peaceful when eating together?*

— *Where and how do they get their grain? Is it on the dirt, in removable buckets, or is the grain dumped in a permanent box?*

— *If grain is dumped into a permanent box, what is it made off? Can it be cleaned easily? Is it being cleaned?*

— *Do you see any rat droppings anywhere?*

— *Are things clean? Is the food stored in animal proof bins?*

— *Do you get the feeling that the barn owner understands horses and their herd dynamics?*

— *Do you get a sense that they are willing to work with the herd dynamics or do they prefer to ignore them?*

11. Manure management...
Can you decipher the barn's dirty little secret?

When I only had three horses to care for it wasn't so bad when it came to picking up the daily manure and dumping it on the manure pile. After a few months and turning it over with the tractor every so often I had about the right amount to put in the gardens and landscaping, and share some with the neighbors. But when the number of horses started to go past that point, the amount of manure collected was considerable and the back yard garden said "enough"!

So now where does it go and how do you keep up with the amount of manure that the horses produce? Because, trust me, it's a lot! This is a real problem that every barns faces. And if it's not dealt with properly you not only end up with more insects and odor, but the environment suffers too.

Some barns will just pay to have it hauled away. This is a very expensive solution and not necessarily an option for all barns. Many just keep on piling it on to the manure pile which just gets taller and wider. Some piles are as old as ten years or even worse.

Others will compost the manure by turning it over regularly and then reuse it as fertilizer on the fields. This is the most desirable route to go, provided the composting process has been done correctly.

If you want to learn more about some of the problems and suggestions of how to deal with the manure, there is a great site at **ManureMaiden.com** that goes a bit further in depth. And there are plenty of other sites on the internet that will give you even more information.

Ask the barn owner what they do with their manure and if they don't get the manure hauled away take a look around. Where are the piles located? Are they close to water streams? Are they covered up with tarps? The tarps inhibit water from getting into the pile and help prevent the pile from leaching the bad stuff.

I like to have my manure piles in the pastures. It's much easier for me to turn them over with the tractor and once composted they're right there ready to be spread over the fields.

Are you noticing a lot of flies? Is there an odor hanging around? This could suggest that the composting process in the pile isn't working properly.

Make a note of the bedding that's being used too. It's not easy to sift out the actual horse manure from wood shavings so a lot of it tends to end up in the pile. Bedding made of wood shavings or sawdust has a tendency to mess up the nutrient balance in the compost pile since it's high in carbon. And in order to compensate you would actually need to add alfalfa cubes or hay to the pile. Too much bedding also makes the composting process take much longer.

Sometimes people use peat moss as bedding and apart from it making incredible horse bedding the compost pile loves it too. Unfortunately supplies are not readily available in our area making it an expensive alternative. I think I'd be using it otherwise. Ideally what you want is horse manure by itself as it has the perfect nutrient balance and produces the purest compost.

The heat inside a properly composting manure pile kills the parasite eggs/larvae and weed seeds. This is one of the reasons why I like the wood pellets so much since it's so easy to sift out the manure. It keeps my piles in much better shape and when you turn it over and put some oxygen back into the mix, you literally see the piles shrink in size. The end result is properly composted fertilizer ready to be spread out over the fields.

As an alternative to picking the pastures, which is a nearly impossible thing to keep up with I might add, people will often drag the pastures with harrows to break up the manure. This is not so bad in hot summer months since parasites don't do well in the heat, but not the best in wet times of the year.

Questions to Ask...

— *What is being done with the manure? Is it being shipped off or composted and reused on the fields as fertilizer?*

— *Are fields being dragged to break apart and spread the manure?*

— *If dragging is the preferred method of dealing with the manure in the fields, during what times of the year is this typically done?*

— *What kind of bedding is used and why?*

Things to Observe ...

— *Where are the manure piles located? Are they close to water streams?*

— *Are manure piles covered with tarps or do they have roofs over top?*

— *Do you notice a lot of flies?*

— *Is there an odor hanging around?*

— *What type of bedding is being used?*

— *Do you see a lot of bedding in the manure pile?*

HOW TO FIND TROUBLE FREE HORSE BOARDING

CHAPTER 3
Your First Impressions of the Barn and Property

Some places you walk into you instantly get this feeling of *"Oh... Wow!"* and other places where you think *"Oh My God!"* Some places leave you with no impression at all. They're just there. Everything seems to be in place but nothing draws you.

So what is it about the *"Oh... Wow!"* vs. the *"Oh My God!"*? What causes us to have these instant gut reactions?

I am certainly attracted to order and cleanliness but my *"Oh My God!"* reaction isn't just for places that are in poor repair or where horses are stuffed together like sardines. Some places are simply very uninviting regardless of how beautiful they are.

It could be a type of car that I see parked in the drive way or the fact that it has big black iron security gates or the number of weeds and garbage lying around, the general dress code, the lack of light... it could even be a narrow muddy driveway that leads me to the barn or just something wrong with the general layout of the property. That first impression is very important.

Make a note of it even if you're not sure why you felt that way. You can rationalize as much as you want why a particular place is the right one for you, but if your gut feeling says otherwise you will be reminded of it every time you show up.

Another thing to keep in mind is that not all barns you are going to visit have been built by professionals. And if they were built by a professional, they may not necessarily have been horse people which means that all the ideas and directions have to come from the owner.

The smaller barns often are owner built or inherited and modified or upgraded. When we bought this property I inherited one of those old buildings. It was a nightmare, but you do the best with what's been handed to you.

In your travels you're also likely to come across a stable or two that has been converted from a dairy barn into a horse barn. Something to realize is that materials and height requirements that are okay for cows may not be suitable for horses. Barb wire fencing for example is perfectly fine for dairy cattle but we know what it will do to our fine skinned speedy partners.

The manure troughs that are typically used in cow barns may not have been covered or filled with concrete. These could create dangerous areas for your horse to get caught in especially in an emergency evacuation.

The indoor arena could be a converted cow barn, so ceiling heights may not be up to par for your discipline.

I bet that some of these things would have never crossed your mind. So, yes, it's important to take a good look around to make sure that the conversion has taken the horse's needs and nature into consideration.

I actually visited one of these and just looking around, these were the type of things that came to mind. When I looked in the indoor arena, it wasn't like I consciously made note of the ceiling height. Instead I felt very crowded by the available space. It just didn't feel right. That's why first impressions shouldn't go unnoticed even if you can't explain them at the time. Make a note of how you felt; you can interpret those feelings later.

Over the past couple of years I've certainly learned that running a horse boarding stable is a huge job not to mention very costly. It's very labor intensive and time consuming and horses are unbelievably hard on their environment.

If you want to make sure that your horse is in good hands and has a safe home it's important that you look at how efficient and well thought out everything is.

Simple things like seeing an ATV to distribute hay, or the distance between the manure pile and the barn, the size of the wheel

▼ *The open, spacious, uncluttered, and horse friendly space makes my barn very inviting.*

barrows and manure forks used, the general organization of tools and shovels, the presence of time saving tools like a stall cleaner, etc. can tell you a lot about whether things will get taken care of or not.

The more efficient a facility is the better it can stay on top of the work and maintenance that needs to be done. Don't be shy about asking questions either. And foremost, don't assume anything.

Roofs, arenas, paddocks and footing need to be maintained and replaced every so often. But these items also have a high price tag attached to them which can become a deterrent in getting them seen to. Extending their lifespan and minimizing the amount of maintenance required is therefore key.

Paddocks and outdoor arenas can last much longer if they have appropriate drainage for example. It will cost more up front, but the investment pays for itself in several ways. Not only will they last longer and are they more useable, but cleaning them has suddenly become easier and therefore faster, footing lasts longer and is easier to keep harrowed and in good shape.

When things are efficiently located, well designed, easy to maintain and relatively inexpensive to fix; the work is much more likely to get done.

If, on the other hand, things are cumbersome, far away, poorly designed or if chosen materials are difficult to work with or replace or downright expensive, it won't get done – it's as simple as that.

1. Common types of siding and their hazards

When I built my barn, my criteria for materials were that they had to be horse friendly, easy and cost effective to maintain or repair. It also had to appeal to me, after all I'd be spending nearly as much time there as the horses. But even as a boarder, my surroundings have always been very important to me.

Metal

Not that long ago I visited a boarding stable where they used a lot of metal siding. In fact, it was everywhere. Metal to me is uninviting, attracts too much heat and is noisy when it rains. I find that most buildings with metal siding just look very boxy and industrial to me. Guess that's just my European background coming through. You may not find it an issue.

When I looked at metal siding I learned that if not installed properly horses could seriously slice their legs or hooves if they got caught underneath any of the edges. Or if a horse decided to kick an outside wall and put a hole in it, the metal could also create some very nasty cuts. To properly repair a hole in the wall, you'd have to replace the entire metal panel. I suppose you could just put a small piece over top to cover it, but that will end up looking like patch work over time.

If metal siding is used on the barn and the stalls have attached paddocks, make sure you check the metal sheeting inside the paddocks. Sheet metal is not very strong so check for damage from horses possibly kicking the walls.

If everything is in good repair, great, but if the walls do look like they have been abused, did any of the metal actually break and are there any sharp edges that your horse could hurt himself on? If there are, check for rust. It could be a sign that it's been like that for a while. And depending on how unsafe it is, it could mean that maintenance and safety are not at the top of the priority list.

Are any of the panels pulling away from the wall? On the bottom ledge, is the edge accessible and sharp? Could a horse get their hoof underneath it? Shoes could also get caught on them and actually pull the siding up and away from the wall. The noise of the tearing or buckling metal could also startle your horse and make the situation even worse.

I purposely didn't install metal siding because this part really worried me. I use hog fuel in the paddocks and the depth changes throughout the year. Also, some horses really get going in them.

When my youngsters come in for feeding they just love to do little drag races with each other. Unfortunately for them I had to put an end to that. My paddocks are just not built for that kind of activity. The paddocks are a good 100 feet long, so they can get a bit of speed going. Just before they come to the barn's edge they come to a sliding stop before turning around. If they missed, those legs could easily slip underneath the siding. And what about those horses that like to dig?

In some cases the metal edge may have a folded lip, but with enough impact, that too would become sharp. I have also heard about protective guards but haven't seen them.

So wood just seemed like a much simpler and friendlier choice to me. I'm sure that manufacturers of metal barns have come up with some solid solutions to deal with these kinds of safety concerns but they are not involved necessarily with every barn being built or converted.

And from a maintenance perspective it's much easier for me to run to the lumber yard and get a new piece of wood than having to order the necessary metal siding, get just the right color and then try to install it. Around here metal is a lot more expensive and that could become a deterrent in getting the panel replaced.

So, wherever you see metal siding used in horse areas, make sure you check the panels for any sharp edges that may be sticking out. Check the lower edges, could horses get their feet underneath them? Do you see a patch work of repairs – at least things are being taken care of; but in the same breath, damage is being done which means horses may be getting injured.

Things to Observe ...

— *Do the walls have a battered look to them?*

— *Is any of the metal bent or ripped? Are there any sharp edges a horse could injure himself on?*

— *Do you notice any rust on damaged pieces?*

— *Are any of the panels pulling away from the wall?*

— *On the bottom ledge is the edge accessible and sharp? Could a horse get their foot caught underneath it?*

— *Do you see a patchwork of repairs?*

Wood

If wood siding is used, check for broken panels and protruding nails. Also, if you see holes in the walls make sure there are no splinters. Ask the barn manager whether these are on the list of things to be fixed. If they don't present an immediate safety concern, they will be very low on the list of priorities.

Keeping up with the beaver-like behavior of horses is exhausting. Short of putting metal edging on everything to prevent chewing, it's a demoralizing battle, especially after you've put a lot of care into building the barn. We like things to look good but horses could care less. And after a while we stop caring too. That's not a happy place to be.

Things to Observe ...

— *Are there any holes in the walls?*

— *Do you see any protruding nails or broken panels?*

2. Different types of roofing...
Do you know how to spot problems and signs of wear?

I still remember the look on a prospective boarder's face when she visited my place the first time and told me how she found her horse that morning.

It was raining cats and dogs that day. Her horse was standing on one side of the stall huddled in the corner with one leg resting. On the other side of the stall it was raining almost as hard as it was outside. The roof was in such bad repair that it provided no protection. Her horse was standing in a soggy mess of bedding and manure.

She told me that the barn owner had made several promises throughout the summer that these things were going to be seen to, but summer had passed and winter had already made its presence known.

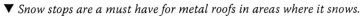

▼ *Snow stops are a must have for metal roofs in areas where it snows.*

Roofs simply need to get done on sunny days. Not only does a roof need to keep our horses out of the weather but it also plays a vital role in keeping the building dry which in turn prevents rot and mold from setting in.

A good roof is essential but too often when barns are built it's done with the attitude "it's just a barn". That attitude tends to transfer into the way a lot of decisions are made and results in many corners being cut, including the roof.

Trust me, I've been there, and I can't tell you how many times I've heard, "It's just a barn" and replied, "Yes, but it's MY barn and we do things right!"

Asphalt Roll Roofing

Before embarking on my adventures with my current barn, we had a rental property that had a barn with a flat roof. I remember putting on asphalt roofing that came in these big rolls. Every seam had to be treated with tar to prevent water from getting in between them. We also had to go back every year and inspect the seams and put more tar on as needed. With the seasonal temperature changes, the tar would become brittle and split. The flat roof made the wear and tear even worse because the water would just sit on it.

Even though it was the cheapest kind of roofing we could get, it was very high maintenance and not a great choice for a barn. And in the end, not very cost effective either.

Metal Roofing

Metal roofing is another favorite choice for barns and compared to asphalt shingles it's more economical. I opted for this one and for the most part it's alright, but there are some things to be aware of.

Metal is an incredible conductor of heat so when storing hay directly underneath it there has to be some kind of insulation to keep it cool. Excellent ventilation is also crucial. Metal is also very noisy in rainstorms and downright loud when it hails, plus it has a tendency to "sweat". Condensation builds up on the inside and it will drip so it is important to have roofing paper directly underneath the metal, at least that's what I decided to do.

Because I didn't like the noise factor and didn't want to be looking at sagging roofing paper or the metal underside of the panels inside the barn, I installed a layer of plywood sheeting underneath the roof panels where the horses live. I love it. It looks so much nicer and makes the barn a lot quieter when it rains.

Even though a metal roof will last more than 30 years, the weak point is in the screws. The screws have rubber grommets to prevent moisture from going down the screw holes. The problem is that with the seasonal temperature changes here the rubber expands and contracts reducing the grommet's life span.

When the snow sits on top of the roof, water will seep underneath the grommets and work its way through the roof. What you call a bad design. And yes, my roof is only three years old and I already have to start thinking about replacing every single screw... the metal is fine!

Thankfully for now this only happens when the snow sits on the roof. When it rains the water runs of quickly enough so it doesn't get a chance to seep through. But I know that I have to deal with this in the not so distant future otherwise it will be raining in my stalls too!

Another thing to keep in mind with metal roofing is that snow will not sit on it. When it starts to melt, it comes off in big sheets and the sound of this really upsets the horses. It also poses a threat to the gutters and the sheer weight and momentum of the wet sliding snow could rip them right off. If the barn has paddocks attached to the stalls, this could be a very upsetting experience. As well, when the snow comes of the roof it will create a bank in front of the stall doors which will interfere with the closing and opening of them.

The sliding snow has caused one of my horses to jump straight out of his paddock. Thankfully he was a darn good jumper and I was right there when it happened. That's when I learned about snow stops. It's a very simple solution to prevent the snow from coming off the roof in these massive sheets. It's a ridge that sits on the roof about two feet above the gutter.

So, when you see a barn with a metal roof, see if they have them installed. If not, see if the barn owner is aware of them and would be willing to install them? They're not that expensive and they sure have given me and my horses back our peace of mind.

Asphalt Shingles

Asphalt shingles are another option and it's the kind of stuff that you'll see on most houses. I like this stuff. It's quiet and doesn't attract nearly as much heat as metal does. There really is no maintenance once it's installed. The downside is that snow just sits on it, but I think after my experience with the rubber grommets, I can live with that.

If you see dark patches on the shingles these could be a sign that the roof is coming to the end of its life. The dark patches indicate that the protective granules are worn off and these are now weak spots. The wind or temperature extremes could cause shingles to curl, and where you have a gap, water has just been given an invitation to enter.

Also check for missing shingles because once any of them are gone, the wind will just start pulling the others away.

So when you're walking around ... observe. Be aware of the condition of things. Look for water damage. Ask the other boarders whether there are any problems with the roof leaking or whether there are any outstanding promises for the roof to be fixed, or anything else for that matter.

Roofs can go for a long time without any problems and are typically fixed only when it simply doesn't do anymore. That's just human nature. But as soon as it starts to leak, they have to be replaced. Unfortunately with the typically large roof surface on a barn, they are very expensive to replace and it's something that has to be build into the budget by the barn owner. If that's not done, these will be left until the last straw is drawn.

And don't forget to look at the gutters! Are they even present? I know these things are hard to inspect from the ground, but if you see a lot of debris hanging over the edges this could be an indication that the gutters need to be cleaned out.

Whether this is an issue will be dependent on the time of year and the climate you live in. Sometimes the down pipes have clean outs making it easy to get rid of some of the leaves and debris. They do help in keeping the gutters a lot cleaner.

◀ *Clean outs are a great help in keeping the gutters clean.*

Things to Observe ...

In general:

— *What type of roof does the barn have? Peaked or flat?*

— *Do you see any signs of water damage?*

— *Check the gutters! Do they look like they're in good condition? No pieces missing? What about the downspouts? Is everything connected properly?*

— *If it's raining, do the gutters look like they function properly or are they overflowing?*

If the roof is made of metal:

— *If you experience snow in the winter in your area, are snow stops installed on the roof? In some climates where there is a lot of snow, gutters are likely to be absent. Gutters are just not designed to take the weight.*

— *When inside the building, can you see the underside of the metal or are you looking at wood or black paper?*

If the roof has shingles:

— *Do you see any dark patches on the shingles?*

— *Can you spot any shingles that might have curled up?*

— *Do you see any missing shingles?*

3. Acceptable ceiling heights

I thought 15.2h was a tall horse until I met my 16.2 and 17.2 Thoroughbreds. Now everyone looks tiny. That equates to 72 inches or 6 feet and that's just their height at their withers! Add some anxiety and they just grew another 4 inches. The 17.2h Thoroughbred that lives at my barn almost touches the top of my 8ft tall stall door frame when standing at the alert with his head raised high. If a horse is rearing, they're taller yet. I think you get my point.

At minimum ceiling heights should be 8ft. My ceilings in the aisleway and hay loft are at 9.5 feet and I actually feel quite comfortable with that. I can even drive my horse trailer into the barn. Because of the design of my barn, the ceilings in the stalls provide even more height.

Horses are claustrophobic by nature so the more space they have around them the more at ease they feel. The minimum 8ft height is applicable to all areas where horses will spend time.

For indoor arenas we have different requirements and the minimum ceiling heights are dependent on what you want to do. For general purpose, a 14 foot clearance will do, but if you're into hunter/jumper you'll want to see at least a 16 foot clearance.

These are MINIMUM heights and are typically applicable to buildings that use conventional trusses because of the "flat" ceilings these create. Personally I would prefer to see at least 22ft before I tend to feel comfortable, but that is me.

If you've come across a facility that has been converted from a dairy barn to a horse barn, then these dimensions are especially important to check out.

4. Lights and electrical outlets... Are they properly covered up?

One place where I boarded had three 60 watt light bulbs in the center aisleway in the peak of the roof. The barn was more than 60 feet long! The stalls had little windows that let in a little extra light but they were quite dirty so they didn't help much. Plus my activities were in the center aisle and light from the windows didn't reach that far.

On a dreary winter day it was really hard to see what I was doing, especially if I needed to attend to a cut or inspect something.

Good lighting is so important. But not only for you; the farrier and vet need lights too.

The interior of a barn is considered to be an outdoor area by the building code, at least in my area. Therefore lights used inside the barn are required to have a weather proof seal. Lights also need to be positioned well away from any possible horse activity. And for added safety, lights should be enclosed in a metal cage. Any exposed wiring within reach of a horse should be run through a

metal or plastic pipe. Some wiring actually has a metal outer casing, so those are okay too.

Horses shouldn't have access to electrical outlets

◄ *Electrical boxes and wires should be covered up, especially when they're within reach of horses.*

either or be able to play with switches. If you see electrical outlets, do they have at least a cover over them? How easy is it for a horse to get to them? Could they chew on them? Because, given a chance, they will.

What about the lighting in the tack room, wash stalls, or grooming and tacking areas? Is it easy to see what you're doing? Are the controls easy to find? What about electrical outlets? Do you see any exposed wires or burn marks on outlets? Burn marks could suggest a faulty outlet or that someone used an old faulty electrical cord.

In wash stalls, do you see outlets that have a little reset switch in them; some may even have a little led? These are called GFCI (Ground Fault Interrupt) plugs and have an automatic shutoff built in. They are required in areas that have water close by.

If you wanted to use clippers could you tie your horse safely near the electrical outlet? Some barns only have one plug as was the case with the barn where I stayed and it was located right by the tack room and nowhere near a safe spot to tie my horse if I needed to.

Things to Observe ...

— *Where are the electrical outlets positioned?*

— *Are there any electrical outlets by the stalls?*

— *Is there an electrical outlet in the tacking area?*

— *Do you see any electrical boxes with wires exposed? Anywhere!*

— *Do electrical outlets close to horses have a cover over them?*

— *Is any wiring accessible to horses? Is accessible wiring threaded through conduits (metal or plastic pipes)*

— *Are any exposed switches accessible to horses?*

— *Are there any electrical outlets in the wash stall? If yes, does it have a reset switch built in and possibly an LED light?*

5. Ventilation...
You can never have enough of it!

When I was thinking of ventilation I was very aware of my hayloft being part of the horse barn. Therefore a great deal of my attention was focused on lots and lots of ventilation.

I've put windows along either side of the hayloft that can be opened, there is a double loft door on either end that can be fully opened, there are another two vents above these doors, there is a solid vent along the full length of the barn on both sides where the wall meets the roof, and there is a large cupola in the middle of the roof.

Hay is stacked 2 feet away from the walls as well. Not only does it give me a path to walk around, it also creates more airflow around the hay. Whenever my hay is delivered, the guys from the hay truck always make sure that the bales are stacked with an air space in between them. I've done what I could to get as much air circulation as possible up there.

But good ventilation isn't only important for hay. Horses need a very well ventilated environment as well.

◀ *Especially in hay lofts, lots of ventilation is very important.*

I remember when in a "former life", my office had been moved into a basement. There was absolutely no air circulation at all and neither were there any doors or windows that could be opened to get some kind of air flow going. It was awful and people were dropping like flies and booked more sick days than I had ever seen in such a short time frame. Including myself; I was constantly sick. And I'm rarely ever sick!

It's not that different for horses when they have to live in a space that doesn't have enough fresh air. Ammonia fumes from the urine need somewhere to go or they'll just linger close to the ground where your horse has his nose while eating his hay.

Bedding and hay attract a lot of dust. These get into your horse's lungs. All this is not only very unpleasant to live in but they can turn into permanent health problems, extended care and ongoing vet bills. Fresh air is an absolute must for any being.

When you walk into the barn, make a note of the smells that come to greet you. Do you get a strong smell of manure? Is there a stuffy feeling? Are you breathing in stale air? Do you get hit with the smell of ammonia or urine as you walk in?

Some barns have large barn doors on either end of the building. When open at both ends, it usually creates good airflow. If you see one side closed, ask why. Not much use if one side is always closed.

If there are windows in the stalls, see if they can be opened. Or if we're into warmer weather, see if the windows are indeed open. Just because they're there doesn't mean they get used.

Look for installed vents in walls and eaves. Ceiling fans are also often used to move air around but you need lots of ceiling height for these. Some facilities have big fans installed in the walls to bring in fresh air. These are effective but could be noisy.

Check the stalls. Is there a gap above the wall that divides the stalls or do the walls go straight to the ceiling? Instead of solid walls, are there grills in place to improve air circulation? The downside with this is that horses will try to play with each other or display aggressive behavior. If your horse is the less dominant of the two, the aggressiveness of his neighbor could add to his stress level.

If hay shares the same building as the horses, look whether the hay area is sealed off to prevent unnecessary dust coming into the horses' area. Since my hayloft is upstairs, I created openings above each stall so I could just drop the hay directly into the stall. Each opening has a sliding door that lets me close it off so dust doesn't get into the horse part of the barn.

Things to Observe ...

— *Is the hay stored inside the same building as the horses? If yes,*

- *Is the hay stored 2 feet off the wall?*

- *Do you see spaces between the bales? The bales of hay should never be tightly stacked.*

- *Does the roof support a cupola or a roof vent that goes the length of the roof?*

- *Is there any venting in the eaves?*

- *Are there doors on either end of the loft?*

- *Are there windows that could be opened up?*

- *Are there any additional vents anywhere? What about wall fans?*

- *Is the hay loft sealed off from the horses' area to minimize dust?*

— *When you walk into the barn, are you greeted with a smell of urine and ammonia?*

— *Is there a strong smell of manure?*

— *Is there a stuffy feeling in the barn?*

— *Are there a lot of flies in the barn?*

— *Are there any large barn doors? Are they open to help airflow?*

— *Are there any windows in the stalls that can be opened? If there is no need to keep the warmth inside the barn, are they in fact open?*

— *Do you see any ceiling fans or wall fans? If they're on, are they noisy?*

— *Do the dividing walls between the stalls go all the way up to the ceiling or is there a gap between the ceiling and the top of the dividing wall?*

— *Is there a grill installed in the wall that divides the stalls?*

▼ *The airspace above my stalls really helps the air circulation in the barn keeping the horses healthy.*

6. Aisleways...
The wider the better.

I opted for a 16 foot aisleway when building my barn and so LOVE IT! And I'm not alone. My boarders, farrier, and vet appreciate it just as much.

In fact, on a dark, wet day my vet drives his truck with mobile lab right inside the barn. Not many places where he can do just that.

Wide aisleways are not common. You're more likely to come across 12 foot wide aisleways but you'll also see 10 or 8 feet wide. In my mind, anything less than 10 feet becomes a safety concern.

In my old barn I have one that's only 7.5 feet wide. Before I completed my renovations in that barn and created a walk through, I always held my breath watching my 15.2h boy negotiate his way around hoping he wouldn't get stuck on something and panic.

▼ *My vet loves the wide aisleway in my barn... and you can see why!*

I have seen some barns where people are allowed to keep tack boxes in the aisleway. Tack boxes are typically 2 feet deep and in a 12 foot aisleway with one parked on either side, you now only have an 8 foot aisleway and lots of obstacles to trip over. With all that stuff around, it's very uncomfortable for two horses to pass, especially when the two horses don't know each other.

And what about stall doors? Are they the sliding type or the hinged kind? Hinged doors typically need 4 feet of swing space for opening and closing.

Another thing to keep in mind is that hinged doors should swing into the aisleway, away from the stall, so that they don't get in the way when you go back and forth. It's much safer this way as it gives you maximum space in the stall and avoids your horse getting trapped behind the door or caught between the door and door frame when leading through. That unexpected "squeeze" can send your horse into a massive panic attack.

When dealing with horses, you simply need space and plenty of it.

Things to Observe ...

— *How wide is the aisleway? Is it a high traffic area?*

— *Are stall doors hinged or are they sliding doors? If stall doors open into the aisleway and stalls are positioned on either side, is there enough room to pass when two doors on opposite sides are open at the same time?*

— *If the barn has hinged type doors, do the doors swing into the stall or aisleway?*

— *Do you see tack boxes parked in the aisleway? If yes, how much available space do you really have?*

— *Can two horses that don't know each other pass each other safely?*

---

7. Floors...
What are they made of and do they provide good traction?

The combination of wet horses, mud, snow, and a smooth surface make for slippery conditions. Add shoes to the mix and things just got worse.

I once watched an old gal of mine come inside the barn and as she made the corner, suddenly one of her back legs slipped from under her causing her to fall down on her hip. I held my breath as she scrambled back up. She was clearly sore and by the looks of it she overstretched a ligament. Thankfully she was much better a couple of hours later but it sure had me worried. It was a miserable day out that day and the humidity and her wet, muddy feet and the rubber mat created an ugly combination.

Center aisles, wash stalls and grooming and tack areas see a lot of traffic but also wet, mud and manure. Anti slip flooring is very important in these areas. If the barn has concrete floors then they should at least have a rough or textured surface on them to add traction.

Often concrete is used in the stalls as well. To provide insulation and added cushioning, rubber mats are typically installed over top. For the most part the rubber mats are fine; however, if humidity is high, the mats tend to "sweat" and become quite slippery. The bedding in the stalls will absorb the moisture though and provide the necessary traction. I use this combination in my stalls and it works well as long as I make sure I have a thin layer of bedding by the doors when it's wet and humid out.

I'd be quite concerned seeing the smooth mats in an aisleway though. There is an anti-slip rubber mat available, but the one I'm thinking of would be quite difficult to keep clean and in order for them to be effective, they would have to be cleaned regularly.

Another floor type that you may come across is asphalt. This type of surface probably gives the best kind of traction for horses. If used in the stalls, they should also be lined with the 3/4 inch rubber mats or at least have ample bedding to give the horses the necessary cushioning.

Dirt is another one I've heard of, but personally I'm not partial to it. It promotes dust, rodents can burrow their way into the ground, and it's difficult to clean. It can be hard to keep level as well, especially when horses like to dig. If you come across a barn with dirt floors check whether the floor is level. Do you see any burrows that could suggest that there are rodents? What is the dust like? How is dust being controlled? Are rubber mats used over top?

In one barn where I boarded they had wooden floors in the stalls. Wood is porous and urine gets absorbed in to the wood and urine odor will be hard to get rid of. If the floor is built with a space underneath it, rodents are likely to create their nests in these wonderful places too. It's also important to check for loose and rotten boards. Your horse's leg could get trapped creating some ugly injuries.

Things to Observe...

— *What is the floor made off? Concrete, dirt, asphalt, wood?*

— *Is the surface smooth or rough?*

— *If it's the main aisleway, is it covered with rubber mats?*

— *If rubber mats are used, are they smooth or made with a special anti-slip surface?*

— *Check the floor in the wash stall. Would a horse have proper traction or could he easily slip if the floor were wet? Is the floor clean?*

8. Organization and cleanliness is key

It feels good to me when I walk into a barn where everything has its place and there is no garbage lying around. It not only points to the general state of mind of the people who run and use the facility but it is also a good indication whether a place is well run or not.

When tools, buckets, wheel barrows, blankets, halters, etc. have their spot it's easier to keep track of what has been done because it all fits within a routine. You're not running around trying to figure out where you have left something wasting valuable time and energy.

Good organization means that not much gets missed and that you can trust that things get done.

If, on the other hand, you see all sorts of stuff lying around or kind of stacked on top of one another or crammed into corners without any logical organization it suggests to me that people either have stopped caring or simply have way too much on their plate. And the associated attitudes, real or perceived, tend to transfer over into the boarders.

Taking care of a boarding stable is a lot of work and when the amount of work gets away on you it can get rather overwhelming. And once we, humans, get overwhelmed, it's our nature to stop doing things.

◀ *An organized tool area makes it easy to find things.*

So, a clean and well organized barn means

- A safe barn
- That the work is likely to get done
- That dust is kept at minimum
- That ammonia fumes are kept at bay
- That we have a healthy environment
- That rodents are looking for a different address.

You get the idea. And of course, cleanliness goes well beyond the boundaries of the barn alone.

Keeping the barn and surroundings clean requires team work. Ask the barn owner what they expect you to do. And for you to do your part, you should have access to a garbage bin, manure pile and the necessary tools to clean up after your horse. Where would you leave the manure after you've finished cleaning up after your horse? What can go into the manure pile and what must go into the garbage?

In spring time, horses shed their winter coats. I don't like having the hair mixed in with the manure as it doesn't decompose well and neither do I want to see any hair around the property. When it rains it becomes a filthy mess, so boarders here are asked to put it in the garbage.

It's the responsibility of the barn owner to make sure that garbage bins are emptied regularly and that garbage is removed from the property, so, while you walk around, check for overflowing garbage bins and overall cleanliness of the place.

If you own a dog and the barn allows you to bring your dog to the barn, you should expect to pick up after him. People like to sit with their horses in the grass to let them graze and socialize with other boarders. They shouldn't have to be looking around to make sure they don't end up sitting in dog poop.

Okay, I must explain ... having lived in Amsterdam for a good 18 years and having to deal with too many oblivious dog owners in a tight space, I know all about its unpleasant, smelly and sticky little surprises... it ain't fun!

Thankfully Amsterdam has since cleaned up its act, but as you can guess I have pretty tight rules surrounding dogs on the property. But if you don't have a dog and are kind of on the same page as me, you will want to ask the barn owner if they have any rules for those who do have dogs. I'll touch on safety issues surrounding dogs, people and, of course, horses later.

Questions to Ask...

— *What are boarders required to do to help keep the place clean?*

— *Are there rules about what goes in the garbage and what can go on the manure pile?*

— *If you were allowed to bring your dog, would you have to pick up after him? Would there be designated areas where he could be or does it matter?*

— *If the barn allows boarders to bring their dogs, what specific rules are there in place for them?*

Things to Observe ...

— *What is your first impression? Are things tidy or do you see "stuff" all over the place?*

— *Do halters and tools have a "home" and do they seem to be kept there in the barn?*

— *Is the garbage can overflowing?*

— *Do you have access to manure forks and wheel barrows to help you do your part?*

9. Places to hang your blankets and halters... Some conveniences are not a luxury.

Having a bracket for a halter and a blanket bar by the stall comes in handy so look around if you see any of these. Where are they installed, could a horse easily get to them? If horses have access to the bridle bracket or blanket bar, are they strong enough to prevent them from getting bend if your horse was to chew on them?

Finding a good sturdy bridle bracket that wasn't too costly was a bit of a challenge. Every store I went to, sold a lighter version which took nothing for the horses to bend and break leaving sharp edges for them to get hurt on. I ended up getting some made that were sturdy enough and now I can finally relax. Horses get into everything and things around them simply have to be solid and strong.

▼ *Holders for saddles, blankets and halters are really nice to have. However, make sure that they don't portrude into the aisleway. Some racks fold away, or in my case, my saddle racks are removable.*

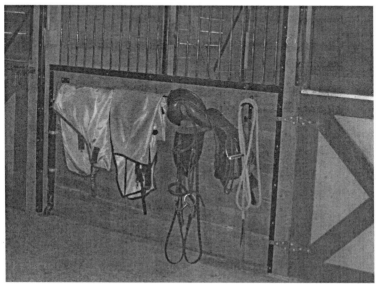

So, when walking around do you see anything sticking out into the aisleway that a horse could get hung up on if he were to walk past? What about the tacking up areas; is there a spot where you can put your saddle and bridle while you're cleaning up your horse?

If you have a wet blanket, is there a spot to dry it out or would you just drape it over the door? In our wet climate here it can be a challenge sometimes to dry out those blankets. A drying room would be something very nice to have, but space and expense prevent this from being a standard feature for most barns.

Things to Observe ...

— *Are there any blanket bars installed by the stalls?*

— *Are they far enough of the ground and deep enough to support a winter blanket?*

— *Are they strong enough to prevent them from getting bent or breaking if your horse were to chew on them?*

— *Is there a bridle bracket by the stall? If you were to try to bend it, does it give easily or are they good and solid? Do any of them have broken pieces?*

— *Can you tell if horses have been playing with them? Look for teeth marks.*

— *In the tacking up area, is there a spot where you can leave your saddle and bridle?*

CHAPTER 4
Is the Place Safe and Secure?

I'm super comfortable with my horse and when I used to board
I was pretty complacent about all the possible things that could
go wrong. When I'm with him, I tend to be in my own bubble. I
don't really pay attention to the other boarders or horses around
me. I guess it's a way of creating your own personal space. I'm just
happily grooming or tacking up and thinking about "stuff". After all
my horse is so well behaved nothing would ever happen, right?

Having been around horses for a long time, I know that an
accident is in a small corner no matter how solid my horse is. As a
flight animal they simply are unpredictable. They pick up sounds
and smells and see things long before we do. Here, if one smells
a bear, the alarm signal is quickly communicated to all those on
the property no matter where everyone is located. The horses are
instantly on the alert and ready to flee.

As a barn owner I'm acutely aware of the things that could go
wrong. I'm responsible not only for the horses under my care but
also those using the facility and the children that come to visit.
If something was to go wrong everyone would be pointing their

fingers at me, rightfully or not, and I could risk losing everything I've worked so hard for.

As a boarder you lose track of that; after all your neck isn't on the line. I know how naive I used to be about all this, but you won't know the true meaning of the other side of the fence until you've walked a mile on that side.

Barn rules are not only there to make sure that a place is kept clean and secure but also to make sure that everyone is safe. If you love the barn where you board, obey the rules because they are there for a VERY good reason.

Even if you are very responsible and careful, if you step out of bounds it only takes moments for someone else who's NOT responsible to copy your actions and put everyone at risk. The effects that our own personal behavior has on other people is something that most of us don't realize.

If the barn rules are not followed, one day your horse may not have a home and you don't have a place to hang out with your friends anymore. So, together, make your favorite barn a safe and secure place.

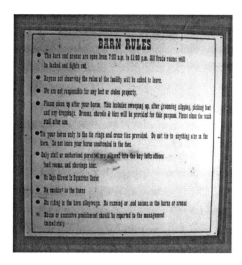

◀ *Barn rules are in place for a good reason. Do your part and obey them.*

1. Safety goes beyond that of your horse

When I thought of safety in the times when I was a boarder I have to admit I only thought of my horse's safety, and things like safe fencing and no garbage in the fields. Of course there are many other aspects to safety that are very important as well.

Having ridden for a long time, a helmet has saved me on a number of occasions. Same with proper foot wear. Eleven hundred pounds on my toes is a painful event, just imagine what it would be like if I were wearing thongs or flip flops! I also like to wear a safety vest when I'm riding young horses or while jumping. That little bit of extra padding goes a long way.

When looking around for a suitable stable I always like to check the barn rules to see what kind of safety rules they have in place. Ultimately it gives me an idea of how serious they are about their business.

But apart from barn rules ... look around ... do you see boarders wearing thongs around horses while grooming and grazing them or riding without a helmet? Do you see horses left unattended?

What about young children? Do you see any running around without any adults nearby? Remember that their loud noises and sudden behaviors can easily startle a horse. And what if the child suddenly crawled under your horse and you didn't know? So, for their safety and everyone else's, children should not ever be left unsupervised when around horses.

Dogs are another big consideration. Almost every horse owner owns a dog and of course would love nothing more than bring them to the barn. But loose running dogs can be a real problem around horses.

I've heard some nightmare stories from friends where a dog started to chase a horse in the arena, throwing its rider and injuring her.

The poor horse was absolutely beside itself and the dog only got more excited just escalating the whole event. The owner of the dog was nowhere to be found.

I've also had people show up and let their dog out saying that he's not a problem around horses. The next thing I know the dog is chasing after a herd in one of my fields scaring the living daylight out of them. After finally getting the dog back in the vehicle it took the herd a few hours to settle down again.

I have also watched boarders trying to manage their horse while trying to discipline their dog from a distance and failing miserably at both. Divided attention around horses is not a good idea and from my perspective as a barn owner, dogs are just an accident waiting to happen if not properly managed.

These things can be avoided with proper rules in place and yes, you may say, "Too many rules make the place restrictive." Perhaps... I would rather look at the flip side and say I have more freedom if both my horse and I can remain injury free. That dog could come after my horse with me on it. No thanks. If rules are common sense then it shouldn't be an issue for anyone to follow them.

Tack up and grooming areas are also common areas for accidents. Horses getting caught in lead ropes left too long, tie rings installed too low, or old and rusty "safety" release clips in cross ties that no longer work.

There should be designated areas where horses can be groomed and tacked up with tie rings positioned at whither height and attached to weight bearing or cemented posts. If a horse were to pull back the tie ring will give before a post gives way. Better yet, use a piece of string as a break away. Boarders shouldn't be allowed to tie their horse to anything they please.

Floors need to be non-slip and clean. Old dropping and moisture create a slippery mess inviting the next accident.

Cleanliness is an absolute necessity when it comes to safety around horses.

On another note, while working on the design and layout of my facility I've come across some ugly stories about barn fires which certainly made me take the safety aspects of the barn very seriously, but I also realized how little attention I paid to these things when I was looking for a place to board my horse.

Where is hay stored for example? The preferred recommendation is to put the hay in a separate building; however, it's not always practical and cost effective to do it that way. When storing hay in the same building as the horses live there are definitely some safety concerns that need to be taken into consideration.

For example, has the hay been tested for moisture content before being stored? Is there a sprinkler system or are there smoke alarms? Is there lots of ventilation in the roof to get rid of the hot air? Is there an air space between the walls and the hay for additional air flow?

In the barn itself, take a look around and imagine whether you could get a horse out easily. Now imagine a horse who is panic stricken with total chaos around him. Could anyone handle him, and where would he be taken so he can run away but still be safe?

Is there an evacuation plan in place? Could the horses be herded out of the barn without tripping over all sorts of things? I've seen quite a few places that allow tack boxes in the aisleway and I always cringe because all I can see is disaster.

And apart from the aisleway being the exit, is there another way out of the stall? Can horses easily get out to the pastures from the barn?

Aside from the horses getting out, can a fire truck get in? Is the road wide enough to allow emergency vehicles to come in? Is there enough space so they can do their job efficiently and safely?

If a horse is injured is there a trailer and truck on site with someone able to drive it? Could a trailer be driven into the barn?

Questions to Ask...

— *What policies are in place about supervising young children?*

— *What policies are in place about dogs on the property?*

— *Is smoking and drinking allowed on the property?*

— *What safety rules do people have to adhere to? Like wearing helmets, gloves, vests, foot wear, etc. Are they clearly posted?*

— *Are tack boxes or any other type of equipment allowed in the aisleway?*

— *Where is the hay stored? Inside the barn or in a separate building? If in a separate building, how close is this building to the barn?*

— *Where does the hay come from? Has the hay been moisture tested before being stored on site?*

— *Is there a sprinkler system installed in the hay loft, smoke alarms, fire extinguishers, fire hose or some other form of fire management?*

— *Where is the nearest fire hall?*

— *Is there an evacuation plan in place?*

— *Is there a trailer and truck on site with someone able to drive it?*

— *Is there someone on site at all times or are the animals left unattended?*

Things to Observe ...

— *Do you see unattended children or dogs running around?*

— *Do you see any unattended horses?*

— *Is the aisleway clear of things horses or people could trip over like tack boxes?*

— *Is there any binder twine laying around that someone could get tangled in?*

— *Are tie rings installed at wither height? Are they attached to weight bearing or cemented posts?*

— *Do the floors have a non-slip surface and are they clean?*

— *Do the stalls have more than one entry?*

— *Do the stalls open up to paddocks? If not, then what do they open up to and is it safe to be used as an alternate exit?*

— *Are paddocks connected to pastures?*

— *Can a fire truck or other emergency vehicle easily get into the property?*

— *In a case of fire could the horses be easily led to the pastures from the barn?*

— *Can the horses be herded out of the barn without being able to get onto the road?*

— *Do you see fire extinguishers, smoke alarms or a sprinkler system installed?*

— *Is there lots of ventilation in the roof to get rid of the hot air?*

— *Do you see birds' nests nestled on top of lights?*

— *Is the barn full of cob webs or do you get the impression that these are being removed on a regular basis? Cob webs are a serious fire hazard.*

2. Security...
We all play a part.

Having boarded at a friend's place for a while, it never occurred to me that there could be concerns around security and that others may not respect my belongings. Not respecting another person's belongings is a totally foreign concept to me. However, once I moved to a different barn this suddenly became a concern.

The tack room was a common room and not secured. Tack would go missing, things were being misplaced or actually emptied, clearly indicating that others were helping themselves to my supplies and grooming aids. And this without being asked certainly left a very uncomfortable feeling.

There was no place that I could call my own and where I could lock things up. The tack room was easily accessible to the general public as well. Entry onto the property was easy and one of my biggest fears would be coming to the barn and find my horse stolen!

▼ *Even a simple gate with a lock on it is enough to keep most unwanted guests out. And the wanted guests, our horses, in!*

Not being able to trust your surroundings and others with whom you share the facility is not a cool feeling.

So, to avoid these worries I look for places that have a secured entry, and I'm fine with it just being a gate with a lock on it. At least it's a deterrent.

I also like to see a lockable tack room or at least individual tack lockers that can be padlocked. As soon as you start to share, you open yourself up for problems and disputes, especially if the barn is open to the public. And if I was to stay at a self board facility, I would like to see at least a storage area for my hay, feed and tack that I could lock.

Another thing to keep in mind is that a private facility is likely to have less traffic than a public facility. Having the barn owner, barn manager or a property manager live onsite is also very important. Not only should the horses be monitored but it also keeps uninvited guests at bay.

I also look at the barn's policy regarding people bringing guests and whether these guests are allowed on the property without the boarder present.

As you can see... lots of things to consider.

Questions to Ask...

— *What policies are in place with respect to boarders and their guests?*

— *Is there a locked entry gate? Are boarders given keys? Is the tack room a shared area?*

— *Is the tack room a locked area, and if so, are boarders given a key or key code?*

— *Are boarders given a separate locker for their tack and supplies?*

— *Are contents in lockers visible?*

— *Can the locker be secured with a padlock?*

— *Do boarders actually lock their lockers? If boarders are able to lock up but don't, you could interpret this as an indication of mutual respect and trust.*

— *Is there a security monitoring system on site?*

— *What procedures does the barn follow when boarders leave? What if a boarder leaves on bad terms? What precautions are there in place so they can't re-enter the premises?*

— *Has a horse ever been stolen from the property? If yes, what happened, what were the circumstances and how was it resolved?*

— *Is there anything in place that can prevent a horse from being stolen?*

— *What will the barn owner do in case there is suspicion that a horse is at risk of being stolen?*

— *Is the facility private or public? Do you notice a lot of people coming and going?*

— *Does the barn owner, barn manager or property manager live on site?*

— *If the facility offers self-board, are you given a personal area for your hay, feed and tack? Can it be locked up?*

HOW TO FIND TROUBLE FREE HORSE BOARDING

CHAPTER 5
Is This a Suitable Home for Your Horse?

My horse being happy when I'm not around means the world to me. To me that means for him to have appropriate shelter, proper day-to-day care and fair treatment, access to fresh water, good quality feed, room to roam and buddies to play with.

Is that a lot to ask for? That depends. When you start throwing your own needs and wants into the mix it gets pretty complex.

Since it's my horse's home it needs to be a happy home for him. After all, he spends all his waking and sleeping hours there. Of course I still need to be able to do the things I love too or why would I have a horse?!

However, in the end it's easier for me to make a compromise than it is for him.

1. Signs of stress...
What do you look for inside the barn?

When horses spend a lot of time in the stalls they are bound to start showing signs of stress and boredom. Turnout is absolutely crucial for these big and beautiful creatures. Even if the barn owner says that horses are being turned out, is it enough? What about winter time? What will the barn owner do if the normal turnout areas are unusable?

There are signs around a stall that can tell you whether horses are unhappy, stressed and bored. A horse that's bored will start to chew on every bit of wood it can find. Sometimes when you walk into a barn and look around you get the feeling that the place was occupied by beavers.

Others may have picked up the habit of weaving back and forth. This puts a lot of pressure on the horse's front legs and knees, and if the weaving is constant, you'll see heavy duty wear marks in front of the door on the stall side. Sometimes barns will put V-shaped grills up to prevent horses from weaving. When you see those, it could suggest that horses spend a lot of time inside and that this is a problem. If the entire barn is outfitted with the V-shaped grills over the door it may just be part of the barn's initial design, but if you see a mixture of stall fronts, I'd make a definite note of it.

If horses happen to be inside while you're checking out the place, see if any are walking around in circles non-stop. This is called "stall walking" and is another sign of stress. If the stalls have vertical grills, horses may also get into the habit of running their teeth up and down the bars NON-STOP.

If you see horses with cribbing collars I would seriously think twice about putting my horse there. It's a horrible habit that other horses are likely to copy. And it's not one you'll be able to get rid of once your horse picks it up. Not realizing what it meant for a horse to be a cribber, I allowed one to stay at my barn. He was an amazing horse and sweet as pie, but he cribbed. Within three weeks I had to ask the owner to find a new home for him. It was like watching a junky. The stress that I felt just watching the poor boy was awful, not to mention the damage he did on my fences and the worry it brought that other horses may pick it up.

When your horse has no stress related behaviors or "vices" you'll want to keep him away from environments that show these types of signs. After all when you see the signs of stress you know that it's not a happy home for horses.

Things to Observe ...

— *When you walk into the barn, do you get the feeling it's occupied by beavers? Every piece of wood has been nibbled on?*

— *Do you see any horses weaving back and forth?*

— *Look inside the stall and see if there are any wear marks in front of the door that could indicate a horse weaving back and forth.*

— *Are the stalls outfitted with V-shaped grills? If yes, have they been installed in each stall or are they random?*

— *If horses are inside, do you see any of them walking around in circles or "stall walking"?*

— *Look in the horses' eyes ... do they look dull and glazed over, or can you see the white in their eyes each time there is some kind of noise?*

— *Look for horses that run their teeth up and down the bars.*

— *Do you see horses with a collar on? If you do, watch them and see if they will grab the top of a board, door, water trough, or anything else with their teeth, curve their neck and pull back and then suck in air. This is the behavior of a cribber.*

2. Smells, dust & ventilation... What are we breathing in?

When walking around the barn, do things smell fresh or are you hit with a strong scent of ammonia? Ammonia is heavier than air and lingers near the floor of the stall. Foals especially spend a lot of time with their noses low to the ground and the ammonia can seriously affect their health. Horses that eat off the ground will also be affected. Strong smells of ammonia means that stalls are not cleaned frequently enough, that ventilation is inadequate, or that the urine gets into the ground as could be the case with dirt floors for example.

Look around for signs of dust as well. Especially in the summer months this will be more of an issue than in the winter. If the bedding is dusty, ask the barn owner what they will do to control the dust. Will they wet down the bedding when it gets too dry?

Some barns like to use blowers to quickly clean the aisleway, but they do stir up the dust. I actually use one since it sure saves time. In my barn I'm not so worried since there is lots of ventilation but it could become problematic if ventilation was compromised.

Questions to Ask...

— *If the bedding gets dusty because of warmer temperatures, will they spray the bedding with water to keep the dust down?*

— *Do they use a leaf blower to clean the aisleway?*

Things to Observe ...

— *When you walk into the barn, do you get a strong smell of ammonia?*

— *Do you see a leaf blower anywhere?*

3. Stalls

The Size of the Stalls

The larger your horse, the larger the stall should be. I don't like seeing a 17h tall Thoroughbred in a 10x10 stall locked up for hours on end. This can happen especially in winter time when turnout is likely compromised and I have seen it happen.

There are a few Things to Consider in deciding whether the stall would be a large enough space for your horse. I think the worst case scenario for any horse is to be locked up for hours in a stall and be dependent on you showing up and taking him out to give him a chance to stretch his legs and breathe some fresh air. I think you'd be stressed to the max as well always worrying about your horse being locked up and being in the dark while it's still light out! At least I sure hope this would bother you.

There are consequences for your horse if he has to live in a stall with minimal turnout. Let me change the perspective a little. Imagine yourself, and I've been there, locked up in a small office, hours on end staring at a computer screen – at least you've got something to do! Your body stiffens up, your legs swell up with water retention and when you get up, your back is sore and you can barely bend or move. And this is worse as we get older. Sound familiar?

It isn't much different for your horse when he's stall bound. Stocking up, for example, is a common complaint when horses don't get turned out enough. Colic is also more prevalent in horses that are stall bound. Add age to the situation and everything gets worse. They have to move, plain and simple.

A stall should at least be 12 ft x12 ft if the horse is 15h and taller. If a horse is stall bound, the stall should even be larger if possible so they can move around. Another thing you need to take into consideration is your horse. A friend of mine told me not that long ago that one of their horses when he'd roll wouldn't be able to get up in a 12 x 12 stall without scuffing up his knees badly. They ended up giving him a nice big 12 x 16 which solved the problem.

Some barns have a paddock directly attached to the stall. This is most ideal I think. It not only gives them more space and the ability to go outside to stretch their legs but also plenty of fresh air.

Questions to Ask...

— *How large are the stalls?*

— *If there are multiple sizes, where is your horse likely to be housed?*

— *What is the base floor in the stalls?*

— *If the stalls have a wooden floor, is there an air space below the floor?*

Things to Observe ...

— *Does the stall have an attached paddock and do horses have free access to it?*

Flooring

As with anything there are plenty of different flooring types. Some barns have dirt floors, others have wooden boards, or the stall floor is simply made out of concrete.

I have only had experience with wooden and concrete floors in barns, but I have heard of people using just dirt for floors as well.

If you see a barn with dirt floors, make sure that the floors are level and don't have holes. With dirt floors I always have visions of rats burrowing themselves in the ground. Also, when horses like to paw, which they do, they can dig some significant holes. To me it just spells more maintenance and I would question that barn owners will stay on top of the care of their floors, especially when they have a lot of horses to take care of.

Wooden floors didn't appeal much to me either. The urine gets into the wood and over time the boards will rot. As well, there is an air space below the floor which to me is another rat's nest I can't get to.

Yes, my preference is concrete, but concrete or asphalt really should be covered with 3/4 inch thick rubber mats and they must be well fitted and lying flat. The rubber acts as an insulator to the cold and damp coming from the ground plus it provides extra cushioning.

One of my boarders told me that with the rubber mats she doesn't worry anymore about her horses when there is a lightning storm, especially with her horses wearing shoes. This was an added benefit I never really considered but she's absolutely right. Electricity doesn't conduct through rubber – much like you driving in a car while going through a lightning storm. The rubber tires keep you safe and so do the mats keep your horse safe.

Rubber mats are easy to clean and don't hold any smells. Neither do you have to use a lot of bedding which saves the manure pile, not to mention flies!

I have been in places where the rubber mats were just bits and pieces and kind of lying over top of one another. A rubber mat isn't THAT expensive and I don't understand that once a mat has had its usable life, why it just doesn't get replaced? A mat can last up to 10 years! To me those are signs that perhaps the facility may be strapped for money, has stopped caring or just has too much on their plate.

In some cases a horse that weaves may be so hard on the mat that they'd literally drill holes in them. Horses with shoes are also very hard on mats, or any surface for that matter, and will cut the lifespan in half. If it's unreasonable wear and tear, then you should expect to receive a bill for things like this.

Things to Observe ...

— *Is the stall lined with rubber mats? If yes,*
  - *Do they lie flat in the stalls?*
  - *Or do you see a bunch of small pieces just kind of spread out and stacked on top of one another?*

— *Do the stalls have dirt floors? If yes,*
  - *Are they level?*
  - *Do you see holes?*
  - *Do they appear to be dug by horses? If you see small holes, it could mean that rodents have created a home there as well.*

— *If the stall floor is concrete or asphalt but without a rubber mat, do they provide enough bedding to add cushioning and protection from the hard surface?*

— *Does the stall have a wooden floor? If yes,*
  - *Do the boards look in decent shape?*
  - *What is the smell of urine like?*

Bedding

There are different styles of bedding practices and depending on the style this may define how much and what type of bedding is used. Cost and availability is another factor. The type of flooring also plays a role and then, of course, there is the personal preference of the barn owner.

To get the full spectrum of different bedding types and practices it's probably better to crack open a book or sit behind the computer and start searching the internet. *The Horse and Hound* has an interesting article about the different types of bedding. You can find it on their web site at **HorseAndHound.co.uk/ horsecare/1370/41386.html**

Some common types of bedding include shredded newspaper, straw, peat moss, wood shavings and sawdust. In my area most people use wood shavings or sawdust (bedding pellets). Peat moss is not common and not that easy to get around here, but it's actually very good for the horses. It really helps their coat and feet. I know of a Thoroughbred racing farm around here that swears by it.

I like to use bedding pellets which turn to sawdust after you add water. It's easy to store and because it's so easy to get the manure sifted out I don't mess up the quality of my manure piles either. Since it's stored in bags and comes in the form of pellets, rats and mice are less likely to make a home out if it as well. There is nothing soft and cozy for the rodents to nestle in like the wood shavings I used to have. That was a big concern for me.

With the rubber mats and attached paddocks I don't need to use much of the bedding either. In the summer months it does get dusty so I take a garden hose to the stalls from time to time and wet it down.

If the barn has a dirt floor, they may follow a practice called "deep litter". I don't have any experience with this approach but if you come across a barn using this method and you want to learn more, search the net for "deep litter management for horses".

Good bedding will absorb the moisture and keep the top layer dry.

Questions to Ask...

— *What kind of bedding is used and why?*

— *Have they ever run out?*

— *And if so, what have they had to do in that case?*

Size and Type of Stall Doors

The minimum size of a stall door opening should be 4 ft wide x 8 ft tall to give the horse ample room to get through without feeling claustrophobic.

Take a good look at the type of doors used and how well they work. A lot of facilities use the grilled sliding doors. In some places where I stayed the sliding doors were in poor condition and wouldn't run well on the tracks making it difficult to get in and out. If the aisleway is narrow (less than 12 feet) and has a lot of stuff piled by the stalls this becomes a safety issue. What happens when two horses pass or another horse has to pass behind you and you're fighting with the door? Anyway, you get the idea – doors should be in good repair and function without effort.

The other type is your standard hinged half door. The door itself should be at least 4 feet tall by 4 feet wide. Make sure the aisleway is wide enough to have a door like this swing open and have another horse pass. Especially if you have stalls on both sides of the aisleway, it can get interesting.

Another thing you might want to look for is whether or not there are latches or hooks to secure the doors when open. Doors that suddenly close on their own as a result of wind blowing through the barn could cause a safety issue.

Things to Observe ...

— *How wide and tall do you think the opening into the stall is?*

— *What kind of door is used? Is it a sliding door or does it swing into the aisleway?*

— *If the stall is equipped with a swing door, make note whether the door swings into the stall or aisleway.*

— *Do the doors open easily?*

— *Are the latches easy to operate?*

— *Is there another entry into the stall?*

— *Are grills installed on the upper section of the door? What kind? Could a horse hang his head into the aisleway?*

Ceiling Heights

As previously mentioned, ceiling heights should be at least 8 feet high, but preferably 9 or 10 feet. A horse hitting his head on a hard surface is a very scary thing to experience and could result in brain damage.

While you're looking at the height of the ceilings, make a quick note of location and position of lights. They may suddenly lower the available ceiling height. Lights should be positioned well away from any horse activity.

My aisleway has a flat ceiling and to keep the lights away from the horses, I opted to have the lights go along both edges of the aisleway keeping the center clear. However, most barns will have them down the center as it's more cost effective. So, as long as the ceiling is high enough, it's not a problem.

Things to Observe ...

— *What is the ceiling height in the center aisleway?*

— *What is the ceiling height in the stall area?*

— *What is the ceiling height in the wash stall or cross tie area?*

— *Are lights or ceiling fans compromising the available ceiling height? Are they recessed or hanging low?*

— *Are lights installed in places that are well out of reach of horses?*

Waterers

How are the horses getting their water? Do they get their water in standard buckets or do they have access to automatic waterers?

If there are a lot of horses, I would hope that there is an automatic watering system. Horses can drink up to 20 gallons of water per day. That is four buckets of water per day per horse! There is no way that a facility can keep up with that kind of demand every day of the year.

If horses are given water in buckets, check out how these buckets are secured in the stall. I have seen places where they use binder twine and tie the buckets to the stall grills, or they may use karabiner clips. Horses will mouth everything and these clips can be an accident waiting to happen.

◀ *Buckets should be securely attached to the wall.*

There are better, safer and more secure methods out there like properly designed bucket brackets. The style I like to use secures the handle and the flat side of the bucket to the wall so it's harder for the horse to mess around with it.

If there is an automatic watering system, take a look at the type used. Usually you will see the ones that are used for cows. They are small and look like a half bowl. On the wall side there is a pedal that the horse has to push in with his nose in order to activate the water flow. The down side with this type is that you can never see how much a horse is actually drinking. They are also difficult to clean out which is a big consideration when there are a lot of them. When something is difficult to do it simply doesn't get done, or at least not often enough.

There is another type of waterer that works on a float valve system. The waterer can hold about 5 gallons of water, the same amount as your typical feed or water bucket.

If they're properly installed you should be able to shut off the water supply to each individual waterer. So if you had to monitor your horse's water intake, you just make sure the bucket is full and turn off the water supply. Once there is no need to monitor him anymore, you just keep the water supply turned on. If there is no easy way to monitor the horse's intake of water, ask the barn manager what they will do if there was a need to know how much a horse was drinking.

Horses should always have a fresh supply of water. When you're checking out the waterers, make sure that they're clean and not slimy, dirty or rusty. Also keep an eye open for waterers that are constantly running or leaking and look for water stains.

I have been in a barn where one of those "cow" like waterers was constantly running. And quite frankly it looked like it had been running for months. I was only there for a couple of days. It was filthy and badly rusted and the only source of water in the stall. The water was running down the wall and the stains told me that it had been like that for quite some time.

Think of the damage the water does to the walls and the floor. What about mold as a result of the constant dampness? It doesn't take that much to call a plumber or put in a new waterer yourself and getting the leak resolved.

And don't forget to ask the barn manager what they do in the winter time when temperatures drop below freezing. Do they have heat tapes installed on the water lines or do they have another system in place to make sure that the horses get the necessary water?

Questions to Ask ...

— *Does the barn get its water from a well? If yes, do they ever run out and what will they do in that case?*

— *How often are waterers thoroughly cleaned out?*

— *What does the barn do to ensure that water doesn't freeze during the winter months?*

Things to Observe ...

— *Is the barn manually filling up the buckets or do the stalls have automatic waterers?*

— *If buckets are used for water, how are they attached to the wall?*

— *If an automatic watering system is used, could you turn off the individual waterer to monitor your horse's intake? Is the bowl large enough to hold enough water to last him for the night?*

— *Do the waterers appear to be in good repair or are they leaking and overflowing?*

Water and Feed Buckets

It's amazing to see what horses can get themselves into. My early lease horse was quite the Houdini and would get into or out of everything if given a chance. His feed and water buckets were always hung on a karabiner clip in his stall.

One morning my friend went to take care of the feeding only to find him standing with his nostril half ripped. He had managed to get his nose stuck in the clip. The vet stitched him back together and once he healed there were thankfully no signs of the awful experience.

That little episode certainly taught me that good solid bucket brackets are absolutely essential!

Now here is another thing I NEVER would have thought could happen. In all the years, I've never had a problem with buckets, but suddenly it happened to me twice within a two week span. Two of my horses got an eye lid caught in the tiny little opening in the loop of the metal handle where the handle attaches to the bucket.

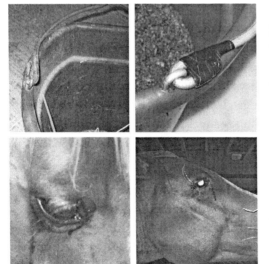

◄ *You'd never think your horse's eye could get caught in the opening. Make sure the ends are wrapped up as shown on the right.*

◄ *Ccino before and after surgery. Thirty cents and 2 minutes of time could have prevented a $500 vet bill!*

The buckets are even supplied with rubber stops to protect the edges and close the gap, but it doesn't matter. When the eyelid gets stuck, the horse panics and pulls back, ripping the eyelid.

My boy shown in the before and after surgery pictures wasn't so bad, but the other horse suffered quite an ugly tear which damaged the eye considerably.

That was a $500 vet bill by the time my boy was all stitched up again. So the thing to do to prevent this is to wrap up the ends of the handles with electrical tape, so that there is no opening for the eye to get stuck in.

Questions to Ask...

— *How are buckets being hung in the stalls? Are they solid and secure?*

— *What type of bucket is being used for water and feed?*

— *Are the "loops" taped up to prevent a horse from getting their eye stuck in it?*

Hay Racks

I have always put the hay on the floor. After all, horses naturally eat with their head down and my horse was always very tidy so I never gave it a second thought. I would just sweep a section of the floor clean so he wouldn't have to maneuver around any bedding and breathe in any of the dust. Unfortunately, or perhaps it's a blessing, God didn't create all horses equal. Some horses are downright pigs and have an all out party in their stall spoiling their hay with manure and urine! Hm.

I've heard of people using hay nets, but there is the danger that your horse can get his feet caught in them, especially when the hay is gone and the netting now hangs closer to the ground. I've always found hay nets hard to fill too, so, not my favorite. I ended up settling for hay racks. It was hard finding a good design though that was deep and would hold enough hay throughout the night. I actually ended up getting some custom made.

When you see hay racks in the stalls, give them a quick look over to see that they're in good repair. Some horses love using them as scratching posts and sometimes they break the welds. A broken hay rack is a quick fix but can easily go un-noticed and leave your horse with an unexpected injury.

Check the height of the hay rack as well. They shouldn't be too high making it difficult for your horse to reach but not too low either where their feet could get caught up in them if they were to kick out or paw.

Questions to Ask...

— *How is hay being fed in the stalls? On the floor, in a rack or hay net?*

— *If a hay net is used, what kind?*

— *If hay is fed on the ground, do they sweep a section of the mat clear so that your horse doesn't have to eat the bedding?*

Things to Observe ...

— *If hay racks are used, are they installed high enough off the ground so your horse couldn't get their legs caught in it? But not so high that it makes it difficult to eat?*

— *Are the hay racks in good repair? Do you see any broken stiles? Check at the weld joints. Those are the weak points.*

Lights and Windows

If the stall doesn't open up to a paddock, does it at least have a window? If so, are there safety bars over the window so that the horse can't get to the glass? If there aren't any safety bars, is the window high enough that the horse can't reach them or instead of glass, is the window made out of Plexiglass? Can the window be opened up for extra ventilation?

If there are lights in the stalls, double check that they have a metal cage around them and are far out of reach of any horse activity, even a rearing horse.

Things to Observe ...

- *Is there a window in the stall?*
- *Is the window made out of glass or plexiglass?*
- *If glass, are there safety bars to prevent your horse from getting injured? Or is it installed well out of reach?*
- *Can the windows be opened for added ventilation?*
- *Where are lights positioned? Could they get in the way of a rearing horse?*
- *Are the lights covered with a metal cage?*

2. Turnout... Is it adequate?

Turnout is the one item on my list that absolutely MUST be part of the package for my horse. The thought of my horse being stuck in a 12x12 stall for 24 hours or more just makes me shudder.

Horses need to roam in order to stay emotionally, mentally and physically healthy. These creatures are designed to travel 20 to 30 km per day in search of food and water and have been quite happy doing it for millions of years.

And now we wish to keep them locked up in a box for hours on end?? And we expect them to be athletes who should be able to perform on an instant's notice after having stood still and unable to stretch for long periods.

When I worked a full-time job and had to commute an hour each way per day I would see my horse three times per week tops. He always had plenty of pasture to roam and herd buddies to interact with and he never experienced any problems that prevented me from going on a trail ride or doing a round of jumps with him. Neither did I ever worry about him going stir crazy and becoming unmanageable. He was simply my happy boy.

Had he been locked up in a stall I would have to see and exercise him every day just to compensate. And instead of owning a horse being an enjoyable experience it now has the danger of turning into a job because if I don't take this seriously he suffers and my pocket book gets hit with vet bills.

The horse's body and circulation depend heavily on the ability to move around. When horses are locked up it lowers their immunity and ability to heal. Digestion becomes less efficient and colic has a much higher chance of becoming a reality.

Walking and grazing keeps the bowels more active and also stimulates the blood flow, and therefore the supply of nutrition, to the horse's hooves and legs. If my horse stocks up or goes lame, it means that I can't take him out for that awesome ride I had promised him. Instead I end up spending more time in the stall attending to his discomfort.

The other thing we easily overlook is that horses kept in stalls don't get the opportunity to interact and socialize with each other. Maybe they can see each other but that isn't the same.

And I'm sorry, even though our horses may think that we're pretty darn cool, we're just not the real deal when it comes to romping around and kicking up our heels!

I have to share a story with you ... I had one owner check out my facility and she told me about her worries and concerns she had with both her horses. The two boys were originally from the track with a long time racing career behind them and had lived in box stalls for most of their lives.

It was winter and the facility where they stayed had lost the use of half of their paddocks due to the bad weather. They did what they could by rotating the horses in and out of the usable paddocks, but it meant that the horses got to be out maybe 2 hours per day if they were lucky.

The two boys could not cope with the lack of turnout and resorted to stall walking and weaving. The owner would rush out to the barn every day, a one hour drive each way, just to get the horses out for a walk and some fresh air.

She was also constantly battling lameness, stocking up, diarrhea and weight loss due to the lack of movement and stress. It's not fun seeing your horses that you love so much in such a state. You do the best you can to help them, and sometimes the only thing you can do is find a different home, which is what she ended up doing.

It was a very tough decision since, after all, you're leaving what's been home to you and you're not sure whether the new home is going to become home again.

Personally, as a barn owner, I like to check the horses before they come to stay with me. So I know the state these two boys were in and the environment they had to deal with. It helped me help them in the transition process when they came to live here.

Here the horses have space to walk and kick up their heels. The transformation in these two boys has been phenomenal. There has been no lameness, no stocking up, no diarrhea, no colic, no stress, nothing. The owner can sleep again at night and doesn't feel like she has to rush out to take care of them.

The moral of the story is really that, unless you have the luxury to be with your horse every day and give him the few hours of exercise and social interaction he needs, you want to make sure that your horse has the necessary opportunities to be a real horse when you're not around.

Be very aware of seasons too. When you look around in the summer everything will be dry. In fact, your focus may be on flies and dust. The muck and mud may not even enter your mind.

Where I live, drainage in paddocks is very important to keep them dry. However, some areas have very high water tables and no matter what you'd do, you could never get rid of the water – where would it go?

Barns that have pastures that are wet in the winter won't allow your horse to be on pasture during these months. This is typically called "seasonal turnout". So, if there is no pasture, where will they get turned out during the day? And how much time will they be spending outside vs. inside!

Paddocks

These are areas where your horse would be turned out when not in a stall. People may also refer to these as sacrifice areas – meaning that there is no grass and instead would have sand, fine gravel or hog fuel for footing. Paddocks may be the only means of turnout, or they are used primarily in the winter time when the pastures are unavailable.

Paddocks come in different sizes and may be attached to the stall like an in/out or be separate and away from the barn. They usually have board fencing, but it will often be combined with electric fencing to stop the horses from chewing on the boards, scratching on the posts, or frolicking with the next door neighbor.

Chewing can be more effectively stopped with metal edging, provided the edging is thick enough. Places may use drywall edging which can be effective depending on how it's been installed, though you'll want to have a good look at it and see if there are any upturned edges from chewing. These become sharp and will injure the horse's mouth.

If the paddocks are away from the barn, they should at least have a shelter. Make a note of the sizes and ask whether the horses are turned out with a buddy or by themselves. There should be enough room for the number of horses that are intended to be sharing that space. How much space is enough? Hm, opinions vary but when it comes to horses, the more the better. My smallest paddock is 1000 sq/ft and that's for one horse. For two horses I'd like to see 1500 sq/ft though one of the real determining factors to the amount of space that two horses really need is their energy level.

As I mentioned earlier, there are different types of footing. Personally I like hog fuel. The cedar keeps bugs away and provides a nice cushy area for horses to lie on and roll. They certainly love the stuff and nothing smells better than a new load!

Hog fuel can have a drying effect on the hooves so you'll need to keep an eye on your horse's feet. When it rains it can hold a lot of moisture so good drainage is very important. Hog fuel breaks down and when it can't drain it breaks down even faster and turns to mud. I have seen paddocks where horses were past their knees in the hog fuel – read major mud and the perfect breeding ground for problems!

You'll likely come across sand and fine gravel in paddocks as well. Fine gravel is easy to clean and both sand and gravel drain really well but they break down and paddocks can get very dusty in the summer. It's also a very uncomfortable surface for a horse to lie on. Another downside to gravel is that it can wear down your horse's hooves too fast. I came across one lady who told me that she had to keep shoes on her horse all the time just so the hooves wouldn't wear down so fast. That's a hefty expense if you don't ride a lot or your horse normally doesn't need shoes, so definitely something to think about. In a place like this, your monthly board just went up.

If the barn uses sand you will need to make sure that hay is fed on a different surface. When horses eat the sand it can result in sand colic. Sand is also known to attract sand flies and some other bugs.

And here is something I would have never thought of!

One of my boarders told me that someone she knew had her horse stay in a sand paddock. After a hot sunny day she happened to look at the underside of her horse's belly and noticed that the entire belly was covered in blisters. The sun had made the sand red hot, and the heat and reflection caused the poor horse's skin to blister.

I was stunned when I heard this, but that sure makes it very clear that the paddock must have a shelter so that your horse can get out of the hot sand and sun. I would even like to see a different kind of material, perhaps even rubber mats in the sheltered area. The sun's changing angles may still be able to get at the sand in the shelter.

Also, before you make a judgment call on the choice of footing used by the boarding stable, keep in mind that it's quite possible that the city has restrictions around the use of hog fuel in some areas so some facilities may not have a choice about the type of footing they put down.

Don't forget to take a good look at the condition of the fencing, gates, and any hot wire that they may have installed.

One place I visited had a lot of paddocks just outside of the barn. I'd say they measured about 30ft x 30ft and housed 2 horses per paddock on average. Nine hundred square feet for two horses is not a lot of space. They all had fine gravel, but looked like they were very ready for a few fresh loads.

It was late winter and there were lots of puddles and uneven ground. The fence boards were badly chewed up and a variety of different types of metal edging was put over top of some sections but not others – nothing looked consistent. In fact, it looked like a real hodgepodge of stuff.

Broken electrical fence wire was knotted back together and left with long strings dangling. Nothing was straight. Replacement boards were just kind of put overtop of broken boards instead of boards taken out and being replaced properly.

To me, these are all signs of not caring or not having enough time or money to do the job properly. It also means that horses are bored and getting themselves into all sorts of stuff.

Questions to Ask...

— *How many horses are turned out together in the paddock?*

— *How large are the paddocks?*

— *How often does new hog fuel, sand or gravel get put in?*

— *How often do the paddocks get the old hog fuel removed?*

— *Is there a drainage system below the surface?*

— *How often are the paddocks cleaned?*

— *Does it get windy on this property?*

— *Where do most of the winds come from in the fall and winter months? (ie. North, East)*

— *What is being done to prevent water from freezing in the winter time?*

— *Who takes care of the general maintenance and repairs around the place?*

Things to Observe ...

— *Are paddocks separate from the barn or attached to the barn?*

— *If paddocks are separate from the barn, how far away are they? Are they easy to get to?*

— *How big are they?*

— *Does the paddock seem big enough for the number of horses that get put in there?*

— *Do the horses have enough room to run around a little?*

— *What kind footing has been used? Gravel, Sand, Hog Fuel? If sand is used, is hay fed in sand or on a different surface like a rubber mat?*

— *Is there a buildup of manure suggesting that the paddocks are not cleaned frequently?*

- *Do they have permanent shelters or are they steel framed canopies?*
- *Do the shelters look to be a descent size? Are they secured to the ground properly? What kind of condition are they in?*
- *If it's windy, are the shelters positioned in a way where the horses are able to get out of the wind?*
- *What kind of fencing has been used? Wood board, metal pipe?*
- *If wood, are fence boards chewed to heck or do they have metal edging to prevent the horses from eating them? If you don't see metal edging, look for signs of used motor oil. Sometimes that's used to keep the horses off the fences but know that it can be extremely toxic.*
- *Do you see any dry wall edging anywhere or rather thin edging? Do you see any edges curled up leaving sharp edges?*
- *Are they using electric fencing anywhere? What condition is it in? Is it powered by solar, battery or electricity?*
- *Do things look orderly and well maintained?*
- *Are there any protruding nails?*
- *Do you see any garbage lying around?*
- *Are the gates in good shape and are they easy to operate?*
- *Are fence posts secure in the ground or do they wiggle back and forth?*
- *Are the water troughs clean and filled with water?*
- *If it's winter and freezing, do you see anything that appears like holes frozen over in the hog fuel? These could be signs of old hog fuel and a paddock in poor condition.*

Pastures

I love watching my horse out in pasture munching grass right next to his favorite pal. This picture stays with me long after I've left the barn reminding me of the beautiful and great day we had. Watching him being content and happy also makes me feel good about the decision I've made about his home.

But it doesn't come without tradeoffs.

In order to want pasture turn out we have to be outside the city limits. If you live in the city this could mean a thirty minute to one hour drive to see your horse. All this time driving seriously cuts into your available time with him.

If we look closer to home, we're starting to find it harder and harder to find places that are able to provide the natural settings that horses really need. The lack of space makes land very expensive and pasture turn out in many areas is simply not possible or largely compromised.

Larger facilities may be positioned on 20 acres and will advertise that they have pasture, but in order to pay for everything they also have 40 some horses in the barn. When you start to dig deeper you

find out that there is only 8 acres in pasture. This shared between 40 horses doesn't leave much pasture per horse.

And what is the soil base? If it's clay, the horses may only be out during the summer months. Then where are they in the winter? And what about giving any of the fields any rest so the grass can grow again?

So, what is really the purpose of having pasture turnout? Is it to feed your horse so he doesn't have to eat hay? Or is it mainly to accommodate his need to socialize, roam and graze and be allowed to be a horse?

Proper pasture management requires rotation and letting the pastures rest. You need space for that. A few horses eat down an acre field in no time flat. The grass can never keep up to their demands.

The amount of grass that will grow is also dependent on the ground. Grass does best in clay based soil and may keep up with the feed requirements of the horses, but in the wet it becomes mud and doesn't make for a good turnout. Horses will have the field destroyed in no time flat.

If the ground is gravel based, it drains extremely well but grass has a much harder time to grow since the soil doesn't keep in the moisture. Gravel based soils though make great turn out areas for the winter. They can take the beating from the horses' feet and because of the natural drainage you don't get the same amount of mud. The harder ground also increases the circulation and blood flow in the horse's legs making their feet a lot tougher.

Properties with clay based soils are likely to offer seasonal turn outs with more available grass throughout the summer months. The quality of the grass is largely dependent on the barn's pasture management practices though. When you take a closer look, some lush looking pastures are full of weeds. And those with gravel based soils are more likely to offer year round turnout but the quality of the grass may be compromised or you may end up with more overgrazed areas and dirt.

For me it's more important that my horse gets to roam and be outside all year rather than have top quality grass to eat. With good quality hay and other feed or supplements you can balance out their nutritional requirements, I think this is easier to do than keeping them confined in small spaces and dealing with all the other stuff that comes with it. That's just my view but this may give you something to think about.

If you're taking a wander through the pasture, make sure that there is no garbage anywhere. My friends have told me some crazy stories of the things they'd come across – car parts, old tires, beer bottles, broken glass, binder twine, you name it.

What about the water supply? Are the troughs clean and filled with water? How is the water kept from freezing in the winter time? Are there any natural water sources? Are they year round, like a spring, or seasonal and are the horses ever solely dependent on them? Are they fresh or stagnant? Stagnant water is a breeding ground for mosquitoes.

Do the pastures have any shelters, either natural or manmade? Check out the condition and observe your own overall impression. How large are the fields and how many horses are typically turned out together? I find 3 or 4 horses on roughly .8 of an acre about the max depending on their energy levels. Any more simply gets too crowded.

Questions to Ask...

— *How large are each of the fields?*

— *How many fields are there?*

— *How many horses are turned out per field?*

— *Are fields given a break from the horses and given a chance to re-grow the grass?*

— *What do they do for pasture management?*

— *How often are the fields dragged or cleaned to control the parasites?*

— *What kind of weed control is used? Do they mow the pastures to keep the weeds down?*

— *What type of grass grows in the pasture? Timothy, clover, etc.*

— *Do the horses have access to the pastures throughout the year or only in summer months?*

Things to Observe ...

— *How far away are the fields from the barn?*

— *Is it easy to get to them? Could an emergency vehicle get to them?*

— *What type of fencing is used?*

— *Are the gates in good shape and in good working order?*

— *Do the gates appear to be horse friendly? No sharp edges for example.*

— *If you see a seriously bent gate which is still being used, does it look like it's been like that for a while? For example, do you see signs of rust around the broken areas?*

— *Is there any garbage lying around in the field, like car parts, old tires, beer bottles, binder twine, or anything else?*

— *What is the soil like – sand, clay, turf, gravel?*

— *Is there actual grass or is it mostly weeds?*

— *Are fence posts secure in the ground or are they loose?*

— *If board fencing is used, is it in good repair? Is it protected with metal edging against chewing?*

— *Are there any protruding nails anywhere?*

- *If wire fencing is used like PolyKote, are the lines good and tight? Are there 3 or 4 rails?*
- *Is there any barb wire fencing used? If yes, is the barb wire located in the busy areas or is it located at the far end of the pasture?*
- *Are there any trees in the pastures that could provide natural shelter and shade?*

Shelters

I rarely ever blanket my horse so a good shelter is important to me, especially if he has no stall for the night.

If a shelter is their permanent home it should be a good solid structure that gives them the necessary protection from the elements. I like the double sided ones so they can pick where they want to be based on what the weather is doing, but these are quite uncommon. The sides should be closed off and meet up with the roof. That way you don't have any chance of rain blowing in.

A good size is 10 feet wide by 20 feet long and at least 8 feet tall at the lowest point. I like to see them outfitted with hayracks and salt blocks. The footing should be dry and well drained. Shelters should be cleaned at least once a week if they're out in the fields and daily in the paddocks.

Steel framed canopies are often seen around here as well. They're a relatively inexpensive solution and still quite effective. However, they really need to be secured properly because the wind will just pick them up like a sail. They also don't withstand the abuse from horses too well and may need to be repaired or replaced quite frequently.

I have seen some places attach sheets of plywood to the sides. Not a bad idea since it gives the structure some rigidity and if done properly they can certainly last a few years and give the horses their necessary break from the rain.

What you do need to watch for is how the canopy has been secured to the ground. I see a lot people bolting them to concrete blocks or tying them to sand bags. Whenever I see this I always worry about the sharp edges of the concrete or objects to trip over.

If the winds are strong, you need some pretty heavy blocks to keep the canopy from moving. How much of a concern this is depends a little on how and where the canopies are being used and whether there are any natural wind breaks on the property.

I would also look to see whether the blocks are completely exposed or closely positioned to the corners of the paddock and by the fence where they are out of the way.

Trees can also make for good shelters. After all, this has been the horse's natural protection from the elements for years! When you

▼ *These canopies make great inexpensive shelters, but be aware of high winds and snow.*

HOW TO FIND TROUBLE FREE HORSE BOARDING

look around in the pastures and there are no manmade shelters, look for good sized trees with a nice canopy that horses can hide under. If you live in an area with four seasons and horses are turned out year round ... make sure the trees are evergreens otherwise they won't provide any protection in the winter time.

Questions to Ask...

— *How strong are the winds that come through the property at different times of the year?*

— *Where do the winter winds come from? East, North?*

Things to Observe ...

— *What types of shelters are there in the paddocks and pastures?*

— *Do the horses have to rely on trees?*

— *Are the shelters positioned in such a way that they will give the horses the proper protection from the winter weather and high winds?*

— *Are things in good repair? Are there any protruding nails? Any broken boards?*

— *If it's a permanent structure, do the outside walls go all the way up to the roof?*

— *Are there any hayracks or salt blocks installed?*

Fencing

As you're checking out the different facilities, you'll be coming across a bunch of different types of fencing. The most common ones that you'll see are wood fencing, PVC planks, high tensile coated wire, barb wire, mesh, or metal pipe. To read more about the specifics, go to **www.PetPlace.com/horses/safe-fencing-for-your-horse/page1.aspx**. They have a good description on each of these, plus list a bunch more.

When I check out the pastures and paddocks, the first thing I look at is the fencing. What type of fencing is used? Is it board fencing or wire like Centaur or PolyKote? If it's wire, how many strands have been installed? Three? Four? Five? This could matter if you were looking for a home for a miniature or pony. If there are only three wires, the mini will get away on you and the pony may too! Has everything been properly tensioned? How are the wires fastened? Does it look secure and safe? Does it look like it would be easy to fix if it needed replacing?

If it's board fencing, are there any broken boards? If there are missing boards, are there any nails that stick out? Are there any nails sticking out anywhere? Do things look to be in good repair? Do things look tidy and consistent or does the fencing look like a mixed bag of things? This usually is a good indication whether maintenance is taken seriously and done with a certain amount of pride or just done on the fly.

Is there any barb wire? Personally I don't want to see ANY barb wire in high traffic areas. This stuff can do some serious damage to your horse. If people make comments like barb wire isn't any worse than wood board fencing, please run.

If the facility uses electric fencing, what kind of charger do they have set up? Is it solar panel or battery operated? If it runs on electricity, is there a backup power supply in case the power goes off? If the fields are gravel based, are there any problems with the electric fence not working?

In order for an electric fence to work properly with ground rods, they need moisture in the ground. Clay based soil contains lots of moisture but a gravel based soil tends to be quite dry and electric fences have a much tougher time maintaining a current. I do believe there is a way around it, but I haven't figured it out yet. Just something to be aware of.

Questions to Ask...

— *Why did they choose the type of fencing used on the property?*

— *If there is any barb wire, will it soon be replaced? When?*

— *If the barn is dependent on electric fencing and it's powered with electricity, not solar, is there a backup power supply?*

Things to Observe ...

— *What types of fencing is used on the property?*

— *If it's board fencing, are there any broken boards? If there are any missing boards, do you see any nails sticking out?*

— *Do things look to be in good repair?*

— *Do things look tidy and consistent or does the fencing look like a mixed bag of things?*

— *If coated wire is used, do the wires look good and tight? Are there any sections not fastened to the fence posts and hanging loose instead?*

— *If electric fencing is used, is it actually transmitting a current? Yes, go touch it! Actually, if you're like me and dread that anticipated shock, you could buy a little fence tester that you sneak in inside your pocket.*

— *Is there any barb wire used on the property? Is it located in any high traffic areas?*

— *Are fence posts secured in the ground or can you wiggle them back and forth?*

Gates

I don't like sharp edges, and my horse and sharp edges are certainly no match made in heaven either. I know some people swear by these metal farm gates that have that folded looking sheet metal. They're called "slat" gates. They have a lot of sharp edges to start with and when they get kicked and buckle, they're even more dangerous.

I've seen one of these used as a main entry gate to a large field with a good 20 horses. We could barely open the thing let alone close it since it was in such bad shape. My friend and I both looked at it in horror. The worst part was that it looked like it had been hit, more than once. And judging by the rust it had been there for a while too. Why wasn't it replaced the first time it got bent?

When you see gates bent and buckled with rusty edges, you can bet that it's been like that for a while. Sometimes gates are held together with binder twine or duct tape.

▼ *The gate on the left still has the ends of the hinges exposed making it unsafe. Make sure that the ends are cut off like the gate on the right.*

When I see this kind of stuff a number of thoughts go through my mind. Are they tight on money? Is there not enough staff to take care of the maintenance? Are they concerned at all with the well being of the horses that live here?

Sometimes, a barn has a number of improvement projects on the go and may not have gotten to this part yet. If other parts of the property look in good repair, ask the barn manager when they expect that gate to be replaced. And, by the way, double the time frame they give you. Stuff always takes longer than you think. Now you need to decide whether you can live with that.

Personally I like the heavy gauge tubular steel gates. They're smooth with rounded corners and when they get hit, they're more likely to bend without leaving sharp edges.

Check how the gates are fastened to the posts. Often you'll see bolts go right through the posts. If that's the case and the bolt ends are on the horse's side, make sure that the ends have been cut off. A horse could injure themselves quite seriously on one of these.

In pastures, the gate areas are also the favorite hangout around feeding time and there is plenty of pushing and shoving going on. It's easy for a horse to get hung up on one of these.

Gate wheels are a great feature. They take some of the load off the fence post and make the operation of the gate much smoother. Something that's quite important when taking horses in and out of the field. Gates are at high traffic areas and the ground gets hit hard with the pounding of the hooves. Are there any signs of gravel to fight off the potential mud in the winter time?

Questions to Ask ...

— *What improvement projects are currently underway?*
— *What is the expected completion time?*

Things to Observe ...

— *What types of gates are used around the property?*

— *Are the gates in good shape and easy to operate?*

— *If the gate is damaged, does the condition of the gate pose a danger to the horses? If yes, is there any rust around the damaged areas that could suggest that it's been like this for a while?*

— *Are there any protruding bolts in the horse area that haven't been cut off?*

— *Are the gates fitted with gate wheels?*

— *Did the barn put any gravel around the gates used in the pasture areas? Horses love to hang out at the gates, plus they are high traffic areas.*

▼ *I love watching the way my mares interact with each other and their foals.*

3. Who will my horse be spending the day with?

My horse is a real social butterfly and he is happiest when he can be out with his buddies munching on hay or having a good game of tag and playing hide-and-seek around the shelter.

He is in a herd that's so cool to watch. I have two two-year old youngsters, a three year-old teenager who is not sure whether he'd rather be grown up or still a kid, and two doting adults. One of the doting adults is my playful boy and he just loves playing along with the kids while making sure they don't get too out of hand.

The other, my more serious boy, has taken it upon himself to keep the kids in line and make sure everyone is fine. If a new baby joins the group, he instantly takes him under his wings and protects him from any uncalled for antics from the others. He makes sure the rules of the herd are passed on quickly and safely and as soon as the youngster has been accepted and found his spot, he just keeps a watchful eye as the world unfolds for this new arrival.

I love watching this little group of geldings. They fascinate me with their rules, their social structure, their ways, and their frolics. They each have their role and together they have such a beautiful balance in their relationships. This is a very happy herd and it makes me very happy to see my horses happy.

Happy herds take time to develop. You have to know the horses on the property well. When a new horse joins the group, I like to take my time to get a feel for him and figure out who may make a good match.

I like to start with horses being fence buddies. If a horse is to join a group, I'll pair him up with one out of the group first – one that I think matches up best. Once the two are comfortable, I'll make them fence buddies with the rest of the group. And if I like what I see, I'll take the new boy on a lead and enter the herd. I'll be there for him and keep the others in line. If things are cool, I'll let him go and watch. If not, we'll go back to some more fence time or find another option.

This is just one scenario. Every horse is so different, and so is every combination. You have to watch the horses and based on your observations, you try different things.

I will often work with the new horse to establish my relationship with him before exposing him to others. He needs to know he is safe with me and that I will look after him. Ask the barn owner how your horse will be integrated in to a herd or introduced to a paddock mate and see how you feel about it.

In some cases, horses will simply be let in to the field without introduction and left to fend for themselves. If the field is large enough it can work, but there will be a fair share of kicking and biting and a higher chance of injury. Horses are pretty rough with each other which can be hard to watch. Once the pecking order has been sorted out again, peace will return.

I've also found that herds of three tend to be less effective than herds of four or more. When there are three, one tends to be spending more time alone or ends up competing for a spot in the group. When there are four or more, they all have somebody to pair off with. Six horses in a group for me is about the max and that's mainly determined by the amount of space that I have available and their energy level.

Sex and age also have to be taken in to consideration. Mares and geldings can mix but when the mares start to cycle, it can really create a lot of hassle, especially in herds with a couple of geldings. Geldings will start to fight over the mares and herd them, leaving the girls no rest. In the winter time things can work more amicably, but the boys will still try to win over their favorite girl. Oh, and the girls can be some incredible flirts too! Sooo … I prefer to keep them separate.

The aging horses also need to be matched up appropriately. They're not as limber anymore as the younger ones and getting out of the way doesn't always come easy and could lead to injury. On the other hand, I have seen the younger ones take care of the older ones and make sure they're treated with respect within the herd. I have also seen older horses come back to life when a youngster joins the group. There is no single recipe here. You have to watch and be aware of what is going on.

And what about stallions? You know what? Every single horse needs a herd in order to feel good, and it's the same for stallions. I haven't dealt much with stallions, but from what I have learned from those that do, stallions tend to do best when allowed to have a normal herd life.

Ask the barn owner how they organize the herds. Do they build herds based on sex, age, pregnant mares and mothers and foals, do they prefer mixed herds or are horses turned out by themselves? Are there any horses with back shoes on?

▼ *Fences give the less dominant horse a chance to escape.*

One thing that can really throw a wrench in to the well being of a herd is a super dominant or aggressive horse that gets on everybody's case. What kind of system does the barn have in place to prevent aggressive horses from boarding there? Will they ask an aggressive horse to leave? Has this happened in the past?

Ask the barn owner who they think your horse may be partnered up with based on what you've told them. Just understand that the picture won't be complete until they've actually met your horse. See if you could meet that horse. As you're walking around the property, are you getting the feeling that the horses are content? Do the horses appear curious and interested in you? Or do they lack luster? Barely pay attention to you? Have a glazed over look in their eyes?

Questions to Ask ...

— *How will my horse be integrated with other horses?*

— *How many horses will they typically put together in a herd?*

— *Do they organize groups by gender, age, pregnant mares and mothers and foals? Do they prefer mixed herds or are horses turned out by themselves?*

— *Do they take in stallions? If so, where do they stay and will they be part of the herd?*

— *Do any of the horses wear back shoes?*

— *Are any of the horses super dominant or aggressive?*

— *If a horse proves to be a problem, what will the barn owner do? Have horses been asked to leave in the past?*

— *Who would make a likely partner for my horse?*

Things to Observe ...

— *Do the horses appear calm, relaxed, and content?*

— *Do you see any of the horses playing?*

— *Do the horses appear curious and interested in you? Or do they lack luster? Barely pay attention to you? Have a glazed over look in their eyes?*

4. Will your horse's day-to-day needs be met?

My boys are very easy keepers and don't need much in terms of blanketing, stabling, medication, and that sort of thing. As long as they have a good shelter, and get a blanket when it really gets cold or wet and a fly mask in the summer months, we're good.

Not all horses are that simple. Some may have day time and night time blankets, or during the summer time they may need a fly sheet. What if your horse requires medication or has other special needs? You need to discuss these kinds of things with the barn owner and see if what you'd like to see happen for your horse can be accommodated.

If your horse is going to be out on pasture, make a mental note of the distance between the barn and the pasture. Is it easy to get to? Is it close by? If it's quite a ways and the fields are large, see if they use an ATV or something to that effect, or just ask what they use to get around? If the property isn't laid out well, and people have to walk great distances to get fly masks or blankets put on or taken off, you run a good chance that it won't get done.

Also ask how many horses live on the property and how many people are there to take care of them. If there are too many horses and not enough people, then things have a tendency to fall behind. You'll also want to check if they have a backup plan in place in case a person can't make it.

With smaller facilities it often is one person taking care of everything. What happens if this person is suddenly ill? Who takes care of the horses? I have 16 horses living with me and one person helping me every morning. It seems to be the magic number for me. Any more horses and I would need to get more help.

The amount of work is also greatly affected by the way the horses are housed and kept. Don't discount the seasons either. The winter months can be far more labor intensive than the summer months depending on how things are organized.

If your horse needs things done mid-day, then a larger facility is more likely to be able to accommodate you since they will have people there on a full-time basis. Smaller operations may only have one or two people taking care of the barn routine in the morning and then again in the evening.

It will be much harder to get these people to commit to mid-day feedings or other things you think your horse needs. Even if the barn owner lives on site, you can't expect them to be on the property 24/7. They have other commitments as well.

Fly Mask Routines

This is a bit of touchy subject for me. I hate it when I see flies in the corners of my horse's eyes or all over his muzzle. Fly masks can prevent infections and, seeing how much more comfortable my horse is with one, I really believe that they are a necessity when we're in the midst of fly season and it's warm out.

Some facilities will automatically put on the fly masks for you as long you provide them. Others will be charging you for each change. Personally, I think this should be part of your horse's basic care.

Billing for each change to me doesn't make any sense and in the end it's your horse that suffers. Fly masks could end up staying on for days at a time, just to avoid a charge or because the barn couldn't get a hold of you to ask whether you want it taken off.

I'm probably exaggerating, and in all honesty I don't have the full context of how this concept works. If the barn can prove to you that this system works, fine, but I would negotiate a flat fee for the month so your horse doesn't end up waiting for your approval to have the mask put on or taken off.

Since at night there are no bugs to fight and the skin needs a break from the straps, it makes sense for the fly masks to come off for the night. It also gives us another check point to make sure nothing has gone wrong or whether the mask was put on too tight.

For a while I leased a horse. Once I bought my own, my available time for the leased horse was considerably less. I would still take the brush to him, make sure he was ok and give him the occasional ride through the trails, but it wasn't enough.

The owner tried out another rider for him to make up for some of the lost time. Since we had to coordinate our days, I knew this rider had been out on Sunday. I showed up again the following weekend – busy week – and went to check on my lease horse. I found him in the field with his fly mask on. His face was very badly swollen; the fly mask had dug right into his skin leaving him with some nasty sores. I couldn't believe what I saw; this kind of damage didn't happen overnight either. What a painful week this must have been for him. I felt downright awful!

The fly mask had been put on way too tight by an inexperienced person, and to boot the barn owner never went to take the fly masks off at night, let alone check on the horses. I was livid, not to mention that I really felt I let this boy down.

That horse eventually became mine, and to this day he still has two little white marks on his face from this incident. These two white marks are two very sad little white reminders for me. The mask was put on too tight and left on. If it was left with enough space it wouldn't have been much of an issue. But the thing that matters more is that the horse should have been checked daily to make sure nothing had gone amiss!

If fly masks are high on your list, make sure you check out the fly mask "policies". I think it should automatically be part of the service, but if not, negotiate a flat monthly rate and put it in writing.

If included, ask them whether they are put on in the mornings and taken off at night?

Questions to Ask ...

— *Is a fly mask service included with board?*

— *If not included with board, what are the extra charges and how are they calculated? Is it possible to negotiate a flat monthly rate?*

— *Are fly masks provided or do I need to bring one for my horse?*

— *Will the fly mask be put on in the morning and taken off for the night?*

Blanketing... Are There Any Restrictions?

With my easy keepers, blankets hardly ever come in to the picture. So if your horse is one of those, special blanket requirements may be off your list too. But if you were moving from a hot to a cold climate for example, then you will have to help your horse acclimatize to the colder conditions with daily blanketing. If there were reasonable temperature differences between day and night, you may have to go as far as switching your blankets twice per day just to keep your horse comfortable.

The same is true if you clip your horse. Since he doesn't have his natural winter coat, you have to compensate with proper blanketing. And what about cold, wet and damp climates? For a horse coming from a different climate these must be the toughest conditions yet to cope with.

Blanketing doesn't only happen in the winter time. Some horses are very sensitive to the little gnats that come out in the summer. These can cause sweet itch and be very uncomfortable to him. In that case your horse may need to be covered from head to toe in a mesh blanket especially designed to protect him against those little biting flies. Blankets that are put on also need to come off again and be put away.

Blanketing is a very time consuming task and you shouldn't expect it to be included with board. If you have special requirements like I just described, you really need to discuss these with the barn owner ahead of time. Also, don't assume that your blanket requirements are "simple" or "basic". I have had people that came to stay here and said that their blanketing requirements were very basic and didn't require any time to do.

It was hard for me to get a handle on what exactly was meant by "basic", and when I started to look after those horses, there was nothing basic about their blanketing needs. It was a major job and an incredible time consumer.

So, don't assume that you're talking about the same thing when you're talking about blanketing requirements. Spell it out. If you don't, you suddenly may end up with either not getting your horse looked after the way you need or you may end up with extra bills that you weren't counting on and that now could put you over your available budget.

Questions to Ask ...

— *Is a blanketing service included with board? Does this extend to the summer months when the flies are out?*

— *Are there any restrictions on the number of changes per month?*

— *What if my horse is allergic to gnats and needs to be covered head to toe during the day; is this included with the offered service or are there extra charges?*

Quality of Feed

I'm a strong believer that good nutrition means a healthy and happy horse. A horse that gets the necessary nutrition is also a horse that isn't hungry all the time. If you were to eat candy bars all day you'd never feel satisfied since your body is looking for the resources it needs to maintain your health and it can't find those in a candy bar. Poor quality feed has the same effect on your horse.

There was one time when I ran out of hay toward the end of the winter. I only had three horses to take care of at that time so it wasn't a big deal. I went to the local feed shop to get a few bales to tide me over until the grass would come in.

This was just locally grown hay and it looked perfectly fine. But after feeding it to my boys for a little while I couldn't believe how incredibly hungry they were all the time. They would just inhale it only to be asking me for more. The hay was clearly lacking what they needed. That certainly taught me that good quality feed is essential and just because it looks good, doesn't mean it's going to leave your horse feeling satisfied.

If you're not familiar with the different types of hay, ask your vet and see what he would recommend. There are certain areas that are known to produce good hay. Find out where these areas are in relation to where you live and then ask the barn owner where they get their hay from.

Questions to Ask ...

— *Where does the hay come from?*

— *Do they use the same grower each time or do they get it from wherever and whomever?*

— *What about grain? How long is it stored before a new batch is brought in?*

Feeding Schedule

Personally I like a flexible feeding schedule. If it's too rigid, meaning that horses are fed exactly at the same time each day, it only adds to their stress if for whatever reason feeding time has to shift. A certain amount of unpredictability is good. My horses are certainly much quieter for it.

You may feel differently about this, so be clear on what you want and why and make sure that the facility of your choice feels the same.

Questions to Ask ...

— *When are typically the feeding times?*

— *Are horses fed at the exact same time every day or is there some flexibility in the schedule?*

Cleaning Routines

I certainly want to see my stalls and paddocks cleaned at least once every day. But it's not only about the frequency of cleaning. What if you have a horse who's bothered with someone cleaning his stall while he's in there? Will the stall hand move the horse to a more comfortable space while his stall is being cleaned out?

Questions to Ask ...

— *How often are stalls, paddocks and pastures cleaned?*

— *Will a handler move a horse to a quieter area if he's bothered by the cleaning of his stall?*

Your Horse as an Individual

The more horses a barn has in their care the more your horse has the risk of becoming a number and being one of many. Each horse is an individual and should be treated as such.

If the barn has a lot of horses in their care, are handlers assigned to certain horses? Watch the interactions between the handlers and the horses. Are horses just moved from one end to another in a rather mechanical way? Observe how the barn owner talks about the horses that live there. There is always a story to tell about the individual personalities of the horses and how they contribute to the overall life at the barn.

If your horse is cold, will they know him enough to be able to tell or even to take the initiative to check on him? A weight tape becomes unnecessary when you can tell whether your horse has gained or lost weight just by looking at him. The same is true when your horse is under stress or hasn't been drinking enough.

When your horse is treated as an individual, you'll know by the comments that are made. One of my boarders always made fun of me because I knew every horse's weight regardless of whether I'd thrown a weight tape around them or not. You get to know their "fat pockets" and general demeanor.

Questions to Ask ...

— *Are handlers assigned to certain horses?*

Things to Observe ...

— *How does the barn owner talk about the horses that live there?*

— *Watch the interactions between the handler and the horses. Are horses moved around in a rather absent and mechanical way?*

— *How does the barn owner interact with the horses?*

Basic Medical Care

Basic medical care should be part of the package. As I've learned over the past few years, even those owners living close by tend to disappear for days on end, just because they can. Cuts, scrapes and sprains happen and they need to be attended to when they happen. They can't be left in the hope that you will show up in the next 12 hours.

So, even with the base level of service, basic medical care needs to be included. Cuts need to be cleaned and disinfected. Sprains need to be cold hosed to make sure swelling is kept at bay. Scrapes need to be checked and quickly hosed off. You just want to be sure they're not deep enough to cause infection.

If cuts and scrapes require more attention than just a quick clean and some disinfectant, you should be notified and you'll need to make the necessary arrangements to take care of your horse. If you live close enough to the barn you can quickly pop over and take care of him yourself. If you don't, is there someone at the barn knowledgeable enough to take care of your horse?

Questions to Ask ...

— *Is this included with board, and if so, what will they attend to?*

— *Are basic medical supplies included?*

— *If you can't take care of your horse, is there someone who can do this for you? Does this person know what to do?*

— *Are there any extra charges?*

CHAPTER 6
Is This a Fun Place for You?

Ok, so I'm happy with what I've seen for my horse, but now what about me? Can I do the things I enjoy?

Since I was a kid I've had many day dreams about me jumping fences, riding a fox hunt, doing an endurance ride, performing that amazing dressage routine to music, galloping along the beach, riding the trails and going camping with my horse. And I'm sure I could conjure up a few more …

All those things I dreamt of doing with my horse are what made me buy my horse in the first place. So, now that I know that he will be fine in this place, is this going to be a happy place for me as well where I can start making these dreams become a reality?

Well, let's have a look …

1. Would you fit well with the other boarders?

For me, moving to a new boarding place didn't come without mixed feelings. I think the biggest fear is to be moving away from home and not feeling at home at the new barn. I have also heard others complain that they never realized how "cliquey" the group would be.

Getting along with the other boarders is very important and in order for that to happen, you need similar interests and values. Feeling like an outcast is no fun. In the end it means that you'll be moving again. Why would you stay at a place that makes you feel unhappy?

To avoid this happening, I will ask the barn manager what people like to do with their horses. Are they into trail riding, natural horsemanship, jumping, eventing, dressage, cattle penning, you name it.

If you are in to dressage you would probably feel a little out of place at a barn that's focused on cattle penning! What is the main focus of the barn? Is the barn focused on competition, are they geared toward family and kids, or is it more laid back and adult oriented?

What about the average age of the group? If you like to have a peaceful and quiet time at the barn you probably wouldn't want to be staying at a place where there are a lot of teenagers and young adults. If you're looking for things to do for your children, then an adult oriented barn wouldn't be too exciting for them either.

I also think it's important to know how long boarders have been at the barn. When people are coming and going it's hard to get a good stable atmosphere. Just when things are comfortable, a new person could disrupt the whole equilibrium. And this will repeat itself each time a new person comes into the mix. It also suggests the stability of the place. When people are happy, they don't tend to move.

So when you walk into the barn, how do you feel? What is your first impression? Do you feel very uneasy or do you actually feel at ease? If there are any boarders, do they say "Hi" or do they walk around with their heads down and do everything to avoid you? Do they offer to help you if you're by yourself? How do they interact with the barn owner? Does it look like there is a good relationship or do you get negative vibes?

As well, observe how the boarders interact with each other. Are they having fun and do they seem relaxed with each other. Listen to some of the conversations. Is anyone speaking badly of another person? Or do they have negative things to say about the barn owner or how the place is run? You don't want that.

For an atmosphere to be good for everyone you should have no backstabbing, have anyone bitching about another boarder, or, about the way things are run.

▼ *A good group means you can share in your activities. Here, a group of us had decided to take our horses camping. It was a lot of fun!*

Questions to Ask ...

— *What do the other boarders like to do with their horses?*

— *How would they describe the boarders staying at the barn?*

- *Adult oriented?*

- *Average age groups?*

- *Family oriented?*

- *Young adults?*

— *How long do people tend to keep their horses boarded there?*

Things to Observe ...

— *How do you feel when you walk into the barn? Uneasy or at ease? What is your first impression of the atmosphere?*

— *Do the other boarders say "Hi" or do they walk around with their heads down and clearly try to avoid you?*

— *Do they offer to help you if you're by yourself?*

— *What is their interaction like with the barn owner? Does it look like there is a good relationship? Or do you get negative vibes?*

— *How do the boarders interact with each other?*

— *Do you hear of anyone speaking badly about another boarder? Or do they have negative things to say about the barn owner or how the place is run?*

2. What about the amenities you'd like to have?

Bathroom or Porta Potties?

I can't tell you how much I hated having to use the stall as a bathroom in the barn I stayed at, especially in the winter time. So, when I built my barn, a bathroom was very high on my list of must haves. If there is a bathroom, check it out! Is it clean and does it look like it's kept that way? Is there a garbage can? Especially for us females, this is essential!

Some places have porta potties for people to use. They can get pretty awful if not emptied and cleaned regularly but, even after holding my breath and getting out of there PDQ, it's still better than nothing. At least the line up goes quickly! Check them out and see what state they're in. If they're near capacity, are they still clean and descent looking? I noticed some people putting hand wipes in them – what an awesome idea!

Questions to Ask ...

— *Is there a bathroom or do they have porta potties?*

— *If there is a bathroom, how often is it cleaned?*

— *If there are porta potties, how often are they cleaned and emptied?*

Things to Observe ...

— *If there is a bathroom, does it look clean? Is it well stocked with soap and toilet paper? Is there a way to dry your hands?*

— *Is there a garbage can? Is it overflowing or tidy?*

— *If there are porta potties, are they well stocked with toilet paper and hand wipes? Do they smell fresh and do they look clean even if the tank is reaching capacity?*

Wash Stalls and Their Condition

If wash stalls are on your list, check the drain and the surface of the floor. One big problem is that people often just hose everything down the drain including the droppings instead of taking a shovel and removing them. This is especially a problem with properties that are hooked up to a septic system. The droppings must be removed or these systems simply can't cope.

And not only that, if people don't clean up the mess, the drains get plugged and we end up with a slippery and dangerous mess. See if perhaps the facility has installed a separate trap for the droppings. I don't know what the solution is to this problem since I don't have a wash stall and haven't had to deal with it. But it would be a worthwhile conversation to have with the barn owner because it's a real problem from what I've been hearing.

The floor in a wash stall must be absolutely slip proof. If the floor is made out of concrete, see if the surface has a rough texture so horses can't slip, especially when wearing shoes. Rubber mats could be slippery too unless they're special anti-slip mats.

Wash stalls should have both cold and warm water. And no, the warm water isn't necessarily just for you. Vets may need to put horses in the wash stall while taking care of them and they often need warm water.

Some facilities may even offer infra-red warming lights to dry the horses, but this is very rare and quite a luxury.

Are there any times during the year when the wash stall can't be used? If the barn is on a well and it's a hot and dry summer, they could restrict the use of water and not allow you to wash your horse.

Does the barn require you to use cross ties in them? If so, is there some kind of safety release in case your horse slipped, or spooked, so you can cut him loose? More on cross ties next.

Questions to Ask ...

— *Are there times of the year when the wash stalls cannot be used?*

Things to Observe ...

— *Does the floor look clean? No signs of old droppings or plugged drains?*

— *Is there a separate trap for droppings?*

— *Does the floor have a non-slip surface?*

— *Is there both hot and cold water?*

— *Are you required to use cross ties in them?*

— *Any other features like infra-red warming lights for example?*

Cross Ties or No Cross Ties

Some barns won't give you the choice. You better ask the barn owner what their policy is. If you have a horse that's never been in them, be very careful about using them. Cross ties can create a very claustrophobic feeling for a horse to the point they will freak out. I've heard of some horrible accidents – anything from horses flipping over onto their backs and hitting their heads to horses slipping on the ground and not being able to get up.

In fact, one of my boarders was in a barn where cross ties were mandatory. Her horse really felt uncomfortable in them and in one instance became quite anxious. The safety releases didn't work since they were worn out and rusty. He couldn't get out and ended up slipping and going down on the soggy floor which had an accumulation of dirt and old droppings. A knife was nowhere to be seen. He couldn't get up but luckily, trusted her enough to stay calm. When he moved his head just enough she was finally able to unclip him. But it was sheer horror that she felt trying to get him loose.

If you like using cross ties and the barn has them, make sure that there is a safety release so that you can free your horse quickly in case he becomes scared. Check and make sure it works – preferably under some pressure. They shouldn't be old, rusty and worn looking. Do you see a knife close by so you could cut the ropes if something happened? If they use chains, I would first ask the barn owner if they'd be willing to change them to ropes. If not, and you're still wanting to stay at this place, make sure there are bolt cutters hanging on the wall.

Better yet, tie a piece of string to the halter and clip the tie to the string rather than the halter. If the horse slipped, at least the string will break. I would caution against using binder twine though. That stuff is incredibly strong and I have my doubts that it will break.

Questions to Ask ...

— *Are cross ties mandatory?*

Things to Observe ...

— *Is the floor clean?*

— *Does the floor have a non-slip surface?*

— *Are the ties made out of chain or rope?*

— *Are there any safety clips? Are they worn and rusty or in good working order?*

— *Do you see any knives or bolt cutters nearby for emergency use?*

Did You Know that Mounting Blocks not Only Save Your Horse's Back but Also Your Saddle?

Mounting blocks certainly come in handy, especially with our tall horses. Apart from making it safer to get on, they also really save your horse's back.

It goes even further than that – they also save your saddle. I never even really knew this until just recently when the chiropractor was out for my boy. With the dominant mounting from the left, we're actually twisting the saddle tree. That's for an English saddle. I don't know about Western, sorry. They are built so differently that it may not be an issue.

A twisted saddle has all sorts of ramifications. It effects how you are seated and balanced on the horse. If you aren't balanced, your horse can't be either. The saddle causes uneven pressure points that create a physical restructuring of your horse's back because of the way it has to compensate for the imbalance in the saddle, and therefore your, imbalance.

Questions to Ask ...

— *Is there a mounting block by the arena?*

Tack Rooms... Are They for Tack Only?

I think it's important to have a spot where you can leave your saddle. It's a lot of weight to be carting around especially when it's one of those heavy weight western saddles! And let's not forget about all your other stuff.

Sometimes a tack room will have lockers built in but in most cases it will have wall mounts for saddles and bridles. If everything is out in the open, take a good look at how things are organized, if at all. You want to be sure that it's easy to find your stuff, that you have a little spot that you can call your own.

The tack room should be neat and tidy. If it's a mess it's easy for things to go missing but also for others not to respect other people's possessions.

How secure is the tack room or can anyone and everyone just walk in? Would your stuff even be safe? What would you like to bring to the barn? Is there enough room to house all of that? How large is the tack room and how many people do you have to share this with? Are you allowed to bring a tack box? Where would it have to go and would it fit?

How easy is it to get in and out with a heavy saddle or would you be tripping over all sorts of things? Is it insulated to keep the dampness out or is there a heater that can be plugged in during the winter months? This will help prevent mold, which can damage the leather, from growing on your tack. Is the grain kept in the tack room? What about mice and rats?

▼ *The tack room in my barn is where my boarders have a personal locker for their tack, blankets, and other gear they need.*

Questions to Ask ...

— *How many people are using the tack room?*

— *How much can you bring?*

— *Is the tack room insulated to keep the dampness out?*

— *Are you allowed to bring a tack box? If yes, where would you have to keep it?*

Things to Observe ...

— *Secured or public?*

— *How is everything organized? Could you have your own little spot or is it a free for all?*

— *Is there enough room for you to store at least the basics?*

— *Would your tack be safe?*

— *How large is the tack room?*

— *Is the grain kept in the tack room?*

— *Any signs of rodents? Look for droppings.*

Lockers... Do You Have Your Own Personal Space?

Lockers don't need a tack room per se; they can also be positioned in a hall way. Lockers can be padlocked and give you your own personal space.

I think they are a great idea and I sure wished I had one when I boarded. However, you will want to make sure that they are big enough to hold your things. A locker should be close to 30 inches wide and at least 4 feet tall. Some lockers may be 7 feet tall; others may be 4 feet tall and stacked.

Find out which locker would likely be yours and if they are stacked, can you reach it or is there a step ladder to help you get access? One thing that I came across and that surprised me a little was

---

a photo of tack lockers that had screened doors. You could see exactly what every person had stored. Personally I didn't care too much for that idea. Especially if I had an expensive saddle, I wouldn't want everyone be able to see it. I wonder why they were built this way; perhaps the photo came from a barn that was located in a much warmer climate where ventilation was more important...

Questions to Ask ...

— *What are the dimensions?*

— *Which locker would likely be yours? Can you reach it?*

Things to Observe ...

— *Does it look big enough for at least your basic gear?*

— *Is it easily accessible?*

Laundry On Site or Off Site?

Some facilities offer laundry services directly on site. That's quite convenient especially when you use a lot of saddle pads and other gear that requires frequent washing. See if they offer a full service or if it's self service. What is included and what does it cost?

If it is self service – and some of these apply to full service as well – are there any restrictions on what you can wash and how often? Do they allow you to wash blankets? Are there times of the year where this service is unavailable? I could see this being the case if the stable was on a well and had to restrict water consumption during the summer months.

What does the self service costs? Is it a "coin" operated laundry service? If so, does it take quarters or dollars, or alternatively is it set up to take credit cards, bank cards, or a stable specific money card?

If there is no on-site laundry service, see if an off-site laundry service visits the barn regularly to pick up blankets and saddle pads.

Questions to Ask ...

— *Is there an on-site service?*

- *What's included?*

- *What does it cost?*

- *Are there times of the year where this service is unavailable?*

- *Are there restrictions on what you can wash? Could you wash your blankets?*

— *Is there a laundry pickup service?*

Things to Observe ...

— *If on-site laundry is offered ...*

- *Is it self service or full service*

- *If self service, is it coin operated or set up to take credit cards or other alternative payment methods?*

- *Are there both washers AND dryers?*

Drying Room for Blankets

In our wet coastal climate a drying room for blankets would be really nice to have. But seeing the space and cost constraints most stables are dealing with, they're not common. It would be worth asking the barn manager how they deal with the wet winter blankets though. Drying these in a damp climate is problematic. By themselves, blankets can take days to dry.

Short of being able to throw the blanket in the dryer at home under heavy complaints from the rest of the household, people may leave them on the horse for the night since then at least they will be dry by the morning. I know, the idea is to give the horse a break, but sometimes it's the only thing that actually works. If it's a decent day out the following day, your horse gets a break from it and he'll have a dry blanket for the next rain fall.

Questions to Ask ...

— *How are blankets dried out during the wet winter months?*

3. Can you do the things you'd like to do?

Ok, so I'm happy with the boarders – I think this would be an okay group to hang out with. Most of the amenities I want are here. Couldn't get them all but at least the most important ones are present. So, now, what about the things I can do here?

Recreational Riding

Since I don't have children and am in my forties, I like a quiet atmosphere that lets me be with my horse and focus on building my relationship with him. I also like trail riding, some jumping and the occasional camping trip – mostly recreational stuff. So access to trails, a round pen and at least an outdoor arena is really all I need. During the winter time it would be nice to have some lights in the arena so I can do things with my horse after work during the week, but I can do without it.

If you're like me then you may be quite happy with a private barn with the basic amenities and close to trails. Maybe just another boarder or two – they may even be interested in going out for the occasional ride.

I like to talk to the boarders and see if any of them would be open to doing some rides together, going camping, or undertaking anything else that I might be interested in. Just because they don't do something now, doesn't mean they may not be interested. It may never have crossed their mind. Besides, it makes the whole experience of owning a horse way more fun when you can share some of these things with others. So, don't be shy!

Lessons and Activities for Your Children

If you have kids you may be more interested in activities for them and, therefore, things like pony club, riding lessons or fun days may be high on your list.

I don't know too much about pony club but I have given horsemanship and riding lessons to both children and adults. Students and parents have shared some interesting stories with me and I can certainly add a few of my own to the pile. Here are some of the things I've learned and that I would be on the lookout for:

Let's say that your daughter wanted to take riding lessons. Find out who would be teaching her. If it's not the barn owner, see if the instructor is around and meet them. What is your first impression? What are their qualifications and what kind of education and experience do they have?

Make sure that you have an understanding of the different qualifications and that you're clear on what you'd like an instructor

to have otherwise the things they tell you will just go right over your head.

Don't forget to ask if they have any first aid. After all, accidents happen. How long have they been teaching and do they

◄ *A Kodak moment... my student's first time cleaning out Kismet's hind feet by herself which was quite the milestone for her!*

regularly attend clinics themselves? What is their main focus – English, Western, or?

Ask them what, why and how they would be teaching your daughter. Do they ask questions about your daughter's previous exposure to horses and riding? Would they do an assessment test to see where she's truly at? Saying what you can do and actually demonstrating this can be two different things.

And will they place her in an appropriate group based on her past experience and current skill level? What about appropriate age groups? If she's completely new to horses, will they start with the ground work and basic grooming and handling skills or do they just focus on the riding part?

Do they use natural horsemanship techniques to help the students build a bond with the horse? Quite often it's about how to groom, tack and ride a horse. But based on the comments from some of my students, the whole aspect of horse handling and how to actually build a relationship with the horse was overlooked in their previous lessons.

One on one instruction is definitely more effective than when you have to share the instructor's attention with other students, but on the down side, private lessons are more expensive. Sometimes they will do semi-private lessons, meaning that there will be two students. This works well too provided that both students have the same skill level.

If the lessons are done in groups, how many students will they teach at any one time? Will an assistant instructor be working with the instructor to help the kids in the group and keep an eye on what is going on? An instructor's attention is quickly divided and it can be difficult to keep up with what everyone is doing or not doing. Especially with a group of beginners, a second set of eyes may prevent an accident from happening. As a student, you could also run the risk of being overlooked and feel like you didn't get any value out of the lesson.

As a kid I never wanted anything more than my own horse. Though in pony club I was never assigned to a particular pony, I certainly had my favorite and would try my hardest to get just that one! The instructors liked mixing us up just to give us a broader experience. And at times I thought it was quite fun, especially when I got the toughest ride. Yes, not much fazed me. A bit of a bolt and a buck just made life more exciting.

On the flip side though, if I got to groom and ride my favorite, I actually had a chance to bond and that certainly meant more. One of my students stopped going to her previous riding school for this very reason. The horse she always rode was leased out and no longer available. She told me how much she hated that. Suddenly a big part of her fun was gone.

When she came here for lessons I teamed her up with one of mine and that was her horse for the summer. She loved it. She got to know my boy and his ways. He got to know her and quite liked her too. I saw how much this meant to her and how it improved her learning. She trusted him and was quite prepared to push some of her own comfort zones even though it was scary at times. Having seen this I would certainly encourage you to ask the instructor which horse they think would be a good match for your daughter. And see if you can meet this horse.

When visiting the horse, make a note of your daughter's size and the horse. Why? Depending on what is being taught, this could be a bit of a factor. Something I learned when teaching one of my girls is that since she was quite petite for her age, it was hard for her to master some of the tasks. She was barely 145 cm tall and 75 lbs. She was learning about grooming, saddling, ground work and riding.

Riding was probably the easiest task, but when it came to cleaning my boy's feet or putting on the saddle it was a major feat. She sure had the biggest smile on her face though when she finally managed to clean the back feet by herself!

At times the ground work proved to be a challenge as well since it can be hard to be where you need to be when there is such a size difference. What that really meant for her certainly became very clear to me when I started to do ground work with a 17.2h Thoroughbred. When his head went high he grew another 12 inches! I had to adjust my entire perspective and body position to get my point across. Things are just not proportioned which adds to the challenge. If the horse isn't 100% safe it could also become a safety concern.

Ask the barn owner if there have ever been any accidents with the students. Do they have liability insurance in case something goes amiss? Talk to the other parents as well. If there was an accident, find out what happened and what the end results were.

Go watch a lesson – do you like the way things are being done? Are the kids having fun? Is there a high emphasis on safety practices? What are the horses like that are being used in the lessons? Are they quiet, easy to handle, accommodating or do any of them appear to be in a bad mood? Do any one of the horses seem bothered, if so is the instructor helping the student to work through it?

Ask the barn owner how often the horses are rotated out of the lessons and taken aside for re-training to make sure they stay safe. Horses that have to do the same thing over and over get bored, moody and become unpredictable. They need a change too and with novices, they get accustomed to pushing the boundaries and not having to behave.

A quick note on ponies versus horses: ponies are certainly better proportioned for kids; however, they are often a lot more feisty than a horse as well. See what the instructor's point of view is on this. After all, they know their horses best.

Apart from lessons, does the barn also organize fun days or shows for the kids? This would give the kids an opportunity to put all the stuff they've learned into practice in a fun and exciting way.

Questions to Ask ...

— *Who is the instructor at the facility?*

— *What are their qualifications? What education and experience do they have?*

— *Does the instructor have any first aid?*

— *How long have they been teaching?*

— *Do they regularly attend clinics themselves?*

— *What is their main focus?*

— *Do they use natural horsemanship techniques?*

— *Would they do an assessment test to see where your child is at?*

— *Would your child be getting private, semi-private or group lessons?*

— *Will there be an assistant to help out the instructor in the case of group lessons?*

— *Is your child matched up with one particular horse or not?*

— *How often are the lesson horses rotated out to get a break or some retraining to make sure they stay safe?*

— *Does the barn organize fun days or shows for kids?*

Things to Observe ...

— *What is your first impression when you meet the instructor?*

— *When visiting the horse your child may be matched with, is the horse proportionate in size?*

— *If you're watching a lesson, does it look like the kids are having fun?*

— *Do you like the way thing are being done?*

— *Is there a high emphasis on safety practices?*

— *Do the horses appear calm and content or do any of them seem in a bad mood?*

— *If a horse is acting up, is the instructor working with the student to get through it?*

Lessons for You

I've worked with a few instructors in the past and some experiences were awesome and others a bit less. What defines a good instructor from one not so good? It doesn't have to be much of a difference, but the difference may be everything.

One of the key things I learned is to be aware of my learning style. Since instructors tend to teach in a style that matches their own learning style, it's important to be aware of how we learn best and see if we can't find a teacher that matches our style. A famous reference for figuring out your learning style is the model used by Myers-Briggs. You can probably find some resources on the net to play with or go to the library.

To give you an example, most people like to know *why* they are doing something before *what* they will be learning is explained. But some people may just go straight into telling you *what* you are going to learn without telling you *why* because the *why* to them is obvious. They may also go straight into telling you *how to* do something without explaining the *why* and *what*.

Personally I need to know *why* I'm doing something. If I don't know *why* I need something why would I want to know *what* I'll be learning? That's just to illustrate a little of how learning styles can conflict and therefore create a disconnection between you and the teacher. If you can't connect, learning has just become that much harder and it's probably better to find someone else.

So how can you get an idea of whether the instructor is right for you? Ask them what and how they would be teaching you. Do they actually have a plan?

A number of instructors that I've had never had a curriculum. They would start each lesson with "what would you like to do today?" Having worked at a school and done some teaching, this just used to baffle me. I would often think, "Isn't that up to you to tell me? Don't you keep track of our lessons? Don't you have a lesson plan?"

In all fairness I can see the flip side too. When we run into problems we often like to run these issues through with our instructor, and that's fine if you're more experienced and know where you want to go.

But when you're first starting out, it's nice for the instructor to take the reins and lead you through the initial steps until you have enough of an understanding and skill level where you can now start to problem solve. After all, the instructor sees the bigger picture. They know how each of the components fit together. When you're first starting out, you have no idea where to start and you probably only have a general idea of where you may want to end up.

Something that has frustrated me in the past is that during a session, the horse may have difficulty with a particular exercise.

The instructor may ask if they can get on the horse and before you know it 20 minutes have past while they're trying to correct or teach the horse with the excuse that they can't stop until the horse gets it. The whole purpose is for me to learn how to correct the horse, and quite frankly, yes, you CAN stop in the middle of an exercise even if the horse didn't "get it"; you just start again. A mental break is sometimes exactly what the horse needs at that time. Allow him to regroup and try again. We're far too focused on the end results and forget to read all the other signs.

Why didn't I say anything? I actually felt kind of intimidated. I'm the student so I lacked confidence in my judgment on what's right or not. But it sure bugged the heck out of me.

I think for the instructor it's sometimes hard too to consciously not switch from instructor to trainer. I've certainly been there, and still get caught out from time to time. However this experience has made me very aware of my responsibility as teacher. So when I do take the reins I do my best to stay focused on showing the problem and giving the student the necessary skills to deal with it. That's what teaching is all about, not?

So the moral of this, if you don't want this to happen, talk to the instructor beforehand and set some ground rules. Make it clear that it's not about training the horse but instead that they have to teach you the necessary skills to get past difficult points.

If your skill level isn't quite there yet to deal with the difficult part then perhaps move onto some other areas until you've gotten better and can try again. Some food for thought here.

If you don't like the instructor at the barn make sure you ask whether or not you can bring your own. But don't be surprised if there are some restrictions. For instance, the barn may require that the instructor is properly licensed and has some kind of liability insurance. Or they may be required to sign a liability waiver, or both.

Also check whether there are any instructors that are not welcome at the facility. Sometimes there could be a conflict of interest or simply a conflict in styles or philosophy.

Questions to Ask ...

— *Who is the instructor at the facility?*

— *How do they teach and would they work on a lesson plan with you?*

— *Could you bring your own instructor? If yes, would there be any requirements they'd have to fulfill like have liability insurance, or specific licensing? Would they be required to sign a liability waiver?*

— *Are there any instructors not welcome at the facility? Why not?*

Trail Riding

I've luckily never had to deal with a horse that was arena sour. I've always had access to trails and they make for a great mental break from the arena work, and not just for my horse.

If trails are important to you, how far do you have to travel to get to them? Are there any trails on the property? Do you need a trailer or can you ride to them? If you can ride, how much road riding do you have to do? What is the traffic like on the road? Are there any tricky spots and where along the way are they?

Take a drive and check it out. Would you feel safe with your horse? Is your horse good in traffic or does he spook easily? Could you ride the trails year round or are they seasonal only? Trails can be too muddy in the winter months or creek beds could rise to unsafe levels.

If the trails led you through farming country, do any of the farms use blue berry guns or other type of things to keep birds off their crops? These devices are unnerving to most horses – even the calmest ones.

What about train crossings, tunnels or underpasses that you may have to go through? Nearby here is an awesome trail ride along the water. The first time I did this ride with my friends, they told me about this underpass below the train tracks that we had to go through. It was more like a tunnel and it had an awesome echo. I held my breath hoping the train wouldn't be barreling over top of me as I was making my way to the other side. Yikes!

Questions to Ask ...

— *Are trails close by? How would I get there? How long would it take me?*

— *Is there any road riding to get to the trails?*

— *Are there any tricky sections on the road I should be aware of?*

— *What is traffic like?*

— *Could you ride the trails year round or is it seasonal only?*

— *Are there any blueberry guns or other devices in the area that could be unnerving to horses?*

— *Are there any train crossings, tunnels, underpasses, bridges or major intersections on your way to the trails?*

Competitions, Events, Etc.

If you like to be involved with competitions or eventing, but the facility that you're checking out isn't a competition barn geared up for all this, check whether there is a competition facility nearby. This of course applies to pony club, 4H, lessons, and all that as well. If you don't have a trailer, is it an easy ride on horseback to get there? If you have to traverse the road, is it safe? Is the road a major artery for traffic? If so, how will you get there?

Questions to Ask ...

— *Is there an in-house schedule of events?*

— *Is there an equestrian center nearby that organizes shows and other events?*

— *Is it an easy ride on horseback to get there?*

— *If you have to ride along the road, is it a quiet or busy road? Is there a good shoulder to ride on?*

You Have a Young Horse and Would Like a Trainer to Help You Out

Ever since I got involved with horses I always dreamt of having my own. It took many years before that moment presented itself. There was this drop dead gorgeous Tobiano paint that I admired every time he ran through the field.

He belonged to the barn owner and I had no idea he was even for sale, let alone how old he was or what he knew. I happened to mention to my friend that I'd love to buy a horse one day. I had a lease at the time, and had a hard time seeing me own a horse just yet. I certainly had every reason in the book of why I shouldn't and couldn't. Then my friend told me that she thought he was up for sale and why shouldn't and couldn't I anyway?

The horse was three and just halter broke and now, six years later, he is one very special partner to me. Many of us will buy a young horse thinking that we can train it, but it doesn't take long before we get stuck and need someone to help us get unstuck. It certainly happened to me.

If this situation rings true for you, then it's very useful if the boarding stable has a trainer on site. If there isn't a trainer could they recommend one? Or, if you didn't feel comfortable using their trainer, would they allow you to bring in your own?

If you were allowed to bring in your own, would there be any restrictions? They may require your trainer to carry their own insurance for example. I know in my case my farm insurance only covers my boarding activity and doesn't extend to trainers conducting their business on my property. If, on the other hand, they are properly insured, then it's not a problem.

Sometimes a stable may not support certain philosophies or it's even possible that some people are banned from the facility due to misconduct. It can happen. So, make sure you ask.

Questions to Ask ...

— *Is there a horse trainer at the facility?*

— *What are their qualifications? How much education and experience do they have?*

— *How long have they been training horses?*

— *Do they regularly attend clinics themselves?*

— *What is their main focus? English, western ...*

— *Do they use natural horsemanship techniques?*

— *Do they have favorite mentors that they follow? Who are they? Are you familiar with them?*

— *If there is no horse trainer at the facility, could they recommend one to you?*

— *Would they be comfortable with you bringing your own trainer? Would there be any restrictions?*

— *Are certain people banned from the facility?*

▼ *My 4 year old girl taking it all in stride.*

HOW TO FIND TROUBLE FREE HORSE BOARDING

HOW TO FIND TROUBLE FREE HORSE BOARDING

CHAPTER 7
Arenas

Arenas are under heavy use and take a lot of abuse so you will want to take a good look at the general condition of them, including footing and possible lighting.

Also, when you're looking at the arenas you need to take into consideration the number of people that are boarded at the facility. If there is one indoor, one outdoor, and one round pen but there are 30 some boarders, the chances of you ever using it by yourself are slim unless you're so lucky to be on an opposite schedule from everyone else.

Make sure areas are big enough so you can still do your thing without running into someone all the time. This won't work for the round pen obviously, but I think that when we look around we often forget that we have to share. I know I certainly did. I'm so used to having the arena to myself that when I walk into a facility looking at the different things I'd have access to I tend to see only myself there, not me and 5 or 10 other people. It's a bit of a mental shift, but it's important to add this to the equation if you want to make sure that you end up in a place that's fun for you.

1. Round pens

Round pens are an awesome tool for working with your horse and I wouldn't want to be without one. If there is a facility that you really like but where they don't have one, ask them if you could put up your own.

This is what happened to me when I bought my first horse. Another boarder and I were really keen on having one and after getting the ok from the barn owner we joined forces on the purchase. We bought one that was made out of metal corral panels and completely portable.

We started off with a 50 foot diameter but found quickly it was too small for our horses. My 3 year old boy was over 15h. A canter was nearly impossible for him with his stride and a couple of times he got caught in the openings between the lower bars.

We decided to get the extra panels and go for the 60ft diameter. It was easy to make the adjustment and it ended up working so much better. We had great fun with it.

When you do something like this though, other boarders will likely want to use it as well. We weren't comfortable with others using it because of possible damage – who would end up fixing it and foot the bill for the repair? The answer may be obvious, but the reality is something very different unfortunately.

We also had liability concerns – my friend was a lawyer, what can I say! There were very few boarders at the place where we stayed so it worked well. By the time I moved to my property, my friend really wanted to keep the pen, so she paid me back my half.

I ended up building my own pen. I couldn't afford the cost of the panels and worked out that it was actually less expensive doing it with wooden boards, just a lot of work. I sure was thankful to have had the experience with the metal one. I knew that the height of the walls needed to be at least 4 ½ feet tall, and that the most effective diameter for me was 60 feet, nothing less.

Having watched my horse getting caught in the bottom rungs and experienced another horse do the same on a wooden built one, I put a good 5 rails without spacing on the bottom part of the round pen. This really prevents the horses from slipping through and getting caught and injured.

I have also seen pens that have slanted walls or even walls that are completely solid and almost 8 feet tall. The height of the walls is to stop the horse from being distracted by outside activities. Personally I much rather have them see and take in everything around them. If my connection with my horse is good, anything else shouldn't matter to him. In the end it really comes down to your own personal preference.

Here are some things to look for when you're checking out the round pen. You may like the idea of tall walls or perhaps you want the angled walls, so this would have to be on your list of things to check out. Also make note whether the round pen is made up of metal panels or if it's a permanent wooden structure.

If the round pen is made up of the metal coral panels, check each of the panels for bent tubes and possible sharp edges and rust. If the tubes are bent but smooth, don't worry, but if you see sharp edges ask the barn owner when the panel will be replaced. The presence of rust can suggest that the panel has been like that for a while which would be a cause of concern for me. See if you can ask the other boarders how long that panel has been like that.

If the panels are of an older type, the connection points could have hard angles or corners. Is there any possibility that you could get hung up on these if something happened? The newer panels are all curved and have no sharp corners.

The metal round pens typically have one panel that contains a gate. You can get these in different sizes but 4 and 6 feet wide seems to be the most common. We had a 4 foot entry which worked fine. Check the height too. The new ones are 8 feet but some of the older ones are 7 feet. If you have a tall horse this could be a bit intimidating to start, but shouldn't really be an issue once he gets used to it. Just something to be aware off.

When the round pen is made of wooden boards make sure that all the boards are in good shape and not rotting through. You also don't want to see any protruding nails, broken or missing boards. The gate should be easy to operate and in good condition. Make sure the bottom part of the pen is closed off so your horse can't get his legs caught. If there are gaps in the bottom, see if the barn owner is willing to close off the bottom to make it safer. Your horse's legs are everything!

Make a note of the location of the round pen. Is it easily accessible? Would the entrance be muddy in the winter and prevent access? Could you access it directly from the arena or do you have to walk a ways before you get there? Do you have to go through other pastures in order to get to the round pen? Is the edge of the round pen bordering a pasture? This could be interesting when horses are in the adjacent pasture. You'll often have an audience, but it will also create distractions for your horse when the others come to visit. Personally I don't mind it since it creates an interesting environment and adds to the training, but you may not like it, so be aware of it.

Finally, ask the barn owner if there are any restrictions or rules that must be followed when using the round pen. Not that I've come across it, but it's possible that they may not allow you to ride in it or work with two horses at the same time for example.

Questions to Ask ...

— *Are there any restrictions or rules that must be followed when using the round pen?*

Things to Observe ...

— *Is the round pen made out of wood board or pipe tubing?*

— *If wood, do you see any protruding nails or broken boards?*

— *If metal, are any of the pipes bent? Are there any sharp edges that your horse could get injured on?*

— *What is the height of the walls? Are the walls angled?*

— *Are the bottom two feet solid or at least closed off so that horses can't get their feet caught?*

— *Is the entry gate in good repair and is it easy to open and close?*

— *Where is the round pen located? Is it easy to get to? Do you have to go through pastures to get to it?*

— *Could you access the round pen directly from the arena?*

— *Would you be dealing with a lot of mud at the entry gate in the winter time that could prevent access?*

— *Is the edge of the round pen bordering a pasture?*

2. Outdoor arenas

Depending on the size of the property, a large arena may not be possible. The average size for an arena is 66 x 130 feet (20 x 40 meters). Higher level dressage arenas are 66 x 197 feet (20 x 60 meters) so if you're planning on doing dressage tests it may be worth looking for this.

I used to ride in a 66 x 130 arena and it gets a little tricky when trying to add in jumps. Not that jumping is impossible, but it sure was a treat when I moved to my place where I had a 90 x 180 foot (27 x 55 meter) play pen. If you're into team penning you'll need something along the lines of 120 x 200 foot (36 x 61 meter). For calf roping you'll want to look for a 40 x 300 foot (12 x 91 meter) layout or 70 x 240 foot (21 x 73 meter) if you have a return chute.

Arenas most often have board fence railings. Sometimes a natural fence may be used like a hedge which is fine, but I've also seen

▼ *My student working on some turns with my boy Kismet in the outdoor arena.*

HOW TO FIND TROUBLE FREE HORSE BOARDING

blackberry bushes which aren't so fine. If a natural fence is used, does it look like it's trimmed back regularly? Could you make a straight line along the barrier or do you have to stay away several feet so you can clear the bushes?

When looking at the board fencing, again make sure that there are no protruding nails; or any broken, rotten or missing boards. Also check whether there is anything sticking out that you could get hung up on while riding. Fence posts for example may be positioned on the arena side instead of the outside. Hey, it can happen.

What about drainage? Most arenas have very poor drainage. Ask the barn manager if drain pipes are installed at all to deal with excess water. Or does the ground naturally drain well? Water that stays on the surface can turn into an ice rink in cold weather.

What about access into the arena? Does it get muddy in the rainy season possibly preventing any access? If it does get muddy, would you be willing to tip toe your way in your riding boots to dryer grounds? I know I used to work my way along the top of the arena fence to get past the wet areas while maneuvering my horse through the mud. Are there alternate areas where you could get on your horse? Are the gates easy to operate while sitting on your horse's back?

Where is the arena located? Is it right next to a field with horses? If so, is there a proper barrier? Sometimes facilities may have a double fence to prevent other horses from interfering with the activities in the riding arena. If the horses are fed lunch is the hay put well away from the arena? If the barn fed the horses anywhere close to the arena side at a time when you go riding, your horse could get quite upset and unmanageable. This can actually create quite a dangerous situation if you're not paying attention to it or don't have your horse's full respect.

This has actually happened to me. I was doing ground work with a rather dominant horse that had been absolutely fine in previous sessions. This time it was lunch time, which I didn't know until I got there, and the other horses were fed in the field next to the arena. Since hay was carted through the arena, some of it had dropped on the ground. This whole picture had set off alarm bells within me, except I wasn't listening!

I could tell he was upset about not getting his lunch but he kept flipping between being ok and kind of not as I was asking him to do things. I watched him like a hawk and in one instance asked him to take a few steps back. He suddenly lunged at me biting me on the upper arm and throwing me to the ground.

The intensity with which he came at me was a total surprise. Clearly it had been building up inside him and what he showed me in his general attitude was nowhere near what he was feeling inside, not even close. This is pretty extreme and not something you're likely to come across, but horses simply are unpredictable.

If people are known to be riding around lunch time, and one of the main fields is right next to the arena all it takes is to feed the horses well away from the arena. Ask the barn owner where they typically put out the hay if they feed a lunch. It's also a good idea to check the feeding schedule and see if you can take this into consideration when you plan your rides. Even a horse who knows that it is lunch time but can't see others eat can be a very crappy horse to deal with.

Questions to Ask ...

— *What are the dimensions of the arena?*

— *Are there any times when the arena may not available?*

— *Is the arena outfitted with drain pipes? Or does the ground naturally drain well?*

— *Does the entrance tend to get muddy in the rainy season?*

— *If the arena borders a pasture, are the horses fed their hay well away from the arena?*

Things to Observe ...

— *Is there a railing around the arena? What is it made of?*

— *If wood board is used, is it in good repair?*

   ▪ *Are boards rotten or in good shape?*

   ▪ *Are there any missing boards?*

   ▪ *Do you see any protruding nails?*

   ▪ *Are the posts positioned on the outside?*

— *If there is no railing around the arena, is a natural "fence" used instead? Does it look like it's been maintained or are bushes growing wildly and intruding in to the arena, preventing you from riding a straight line?*

— *Do any of the arena edges border a pasture?*

— *Are gates easy to operate? Could you operate them from your horse's back?*

3. Indoor arenas

I've never had the luxury of an indoor arena at the barn, but when I attend a clinic on a hot day or in the middle of the winter, I sure appreciate it.

When I'd be attending a clinic, it meant that during those times the arena wasn't available for those that boarded there. I always wondered how people felt about this. What about all these strangers taking over their "space"?

My clinic would last four days and I would see the next clinic already advertised on the board for the next weekend. In the summer I don't think it would be such a big deal since there were plenty of other areas for people to go to, however, on a miserable day it meant you were either wearing your tall rubber boots and yellow slickers or stayed at home while those attending the clinic played with their horses and stayed dry.

The summer is one thing but in the winter time I would certainly want to stay out of the elements while having some fun with my horse and I wouldn't be all too thrilled about having to share that space with outsiders. After all, didn't I decide to board at this place because they had an indoor?

In all fairness to the barn, they have to make a living too and by putting on events the facility can generate the much needed cash to keep things running. However, if you're not in to this, check with the barn owner which events are being sponsored by the barn and if there are scheduled times that the indoor wouldn't be available. Is there a schedule that you could take with you? At least you'll be forewarned and can you make an educated decision. Of course, if the events are exactly what you're looking for, then perfect!

Another thing to consider is whether the barn has a breeding program and/or is in the business of training and selling horses.

They too will be using the indoor arena. Are there any particular times when they do this? Do they close off the arena to the other boarders when they are using it? Just something to think about.

When it comes to dimensions, the information is much the same as we covered for the outdoor arenas. However there are different methods of constructing the massive span that these buildings have to accommodate to support the roof.

The most common one is built with the traditional roof trusses. With these you'll want to be sure to check the ceiling height since the trusses take up all the air space below the roof and you'll actually have a "flat" ceiling.

For general use you can get away with 14 foot high ceilings, but when you're getting into hunter/jumper you'll want to make sure that the arena sports at least 16 feet. These are minimum heights by the way.

With clear span structures, like CoverAll, we get to use the entire air space below the ceiling. Ceiling heights are therefore not an issue. These types of buildings certainly create a very nice open and spacious feeling. They are typically white and therefore very bright. If any lights are used they will just reflect off the walls making it even brighter.

In the traditional arenas I've always felt a little claustrophobic since light would really get absorbed by the surroundings. Lighting fixtures tend to be of older types as well and don't emit as many lumens as the new ones. It just makes it harder to see, especially when you have aging eyes. One thing I have noticed though with the CoverAll style buildings is that there is a lot of condensation on the inside. So you may think you're getting out of the rain only to find yourself getting dripped on inside!

Indoor arenas may be completely enclosed; others may have all sides open, also called California style, or just have one side open.

The fully enclosed ones I tend to find stuffy, unless they are built with the clear span structure. You need airflow. Plus on a nice summer day I don't like the feeling of being locked up inside, but that's just me.

The partially enclosed ones I find much more pleasant but you'll want to check that the closed walls are placed where the prevailing winds come from, usually north and north east. See if there is a tree line to provide some added protection. If the indoor arena is built with a CoverAll, see if there are doors on the sides that could be opened up in the summer time for ventilation.

Sometimes the building may not have any ends in place. This is perfectly fine but high winds could create a wind tunnel depending on how the structure has been positioned.

If you live in an area where summers are hot then the California style covered arenas would keep you out of the blistering sun and

▼ *A CoverAll arena leaves a spacious feeling and is bright!*

give you much needed shade. The open sides would allow for excellent circulation keeping it cool under the roof. Ask the other boarders how they like the indoor and if there are any times of the year or certain conditions when it's not so comfortable in there.

Some facilities have the barn incorporated with the arena area. The stalls are kept either separate or may be in the same common area as the indoor in which case the arena and stalls are separated by an aisleway. Even though this last option is kind of cool, I mean I've always liked looking at the horses, but the arena dust really needs to be controlled properly. Otherwise your horse could end up with a respiratory problem for life.

For some horses the activity in the arena could be entertaining but it can also have quite the opposite effect. Horses by nature don't like loud noises and if clinics are being held regularly in the arena, the use of a PA system and people talking and the presence of kids and possibly dogs is just way too much stimulation for them.

Now what about you when you're riding in the arena? All the activity around the horses like cleaning stalls, grooming, tacking up, and horses walking up and down the aisleway can be very distracting for you too. If you're trying to perfect a certain skill you want to be able to concentrate. You'll need to figure out whether or not you can block out all the distractions.

If you see a balustrade or railing separating the aisleway from the arena area, are people hanging their blankets, saddles and other stuff over it? It's a natural thing to do but all this extra stuff could interfere with you in the arena.

Questions to Ask ...

— *What are the dimensions of the arena?*

— *How frequently are clinics or events scheduled to use the indoor? Do they have a schedule?*

— *Are there specific times when the indoor is unavailable?*

Things to Observe ...

— *Is it a clear span structure or do you see trusses?*

— *If trusses, does it look like you have at least 16 feet of clearance?*

— *Is there enough light for you to see what you're doing?*

— *If there are only one or two walls and the rest is open, are the walls positioned on the sides where the prevailing winds come from? In my area these typically come from the North and East.*

— *Is there a tree line that could provide some extra protection?*

— *Can the building be opened up in the summer to provide extra ventilation?*

— *Do stalls share the same space as the arena? Can the arena area be isolated from the stall area to avoid dust?*

4. Footing...
Is it actually safe and functional?

The most common material you're likely to come across is sand. This can either be straight sand or sand mixed with a variety of other materials – like rubber – to add cushioning and spring, retain moisture and to slow the process of breaking down. Sand that breaks down becomes very dusty and is very bad for your lungs and those of your horse.

In indoor arenas, and outdoor too during summer months, it's important that there is some kind of irrigation system installed to wet down the footing to prevent the dust. There are agents that can be added to the sand to hold onto the moisture. Sometimes facilities may use magnesium chloride, but be aware that magnesium chloride has a drying effect on your horse's hooves.

Some agents need to be added every 6 to 12 months depending on how much the arena is being used and also may require the arena be harrowed on a regular basis. Ask the barn manager how they deal with the dust in their arenas and then ask the boarders if they have any issues with dust and whether the arena is harrowed on a regular basis.

I use hog fuel in my outdoor arena. For the most part I quite like this stuff. It smells nice, lasts quite long, is not overly expensive, and more so it gives a nice cushy ride and provides a soft landing for those unfortunate moments.

The downside to hog fuel is that it holds a lot of moisture and as it breaks down you can end up with real soft spots, or holes, in the arena. With this stuff you need excellent drainage whether it be drain pipes or a naturally draining soil.

In the summer months after a heavy rain fall the arena area could become quite warm and humid because of the moisture it holds.

It takes a bit for this stuff to dry out. Ask the barn owner if there is any drainage below the surface? When was the hog fuel last replaced? Take a walk through the arena – do you see any "sink" holes or soft spots?

Another possible sign of old footing is when, in the winter time, you see holes that are frozen over. If the horse steps in to these the ice can be quite sharp and leave the horse with cuts. If it's an outside arena is it usable in the winter months? How often is the arena harrowed to even out the surface and possible holes?

Questions to Ask ...

— *What kind of footing is used? Hog fuel, sand or sand mixture?*

— *Is there an irrigation system installed to deal with dust?*

— *Do they use any agents like magnesium chloride to hold in the moisture?*

— *How often is the arena harrowed?*

— *How often is the footing redressed or replaced?*

— *Is the outdoor arena usable in the winter months?*

Things to Observe ...

— *If the arena uses hog fuel, do you see any sink holes?*

— *If it's winter, do you see any holes frozen over?*

5. Arena lighting...
Can you see what you are doing?

Indoor arenas by standard are equipped with lights and tend to be lit quite consistently from one to another. However, lights are not all that common for outdoor arenas.

I have to warn you that while a facility may advertise "lit arena" that lighting options can take on some creative forms and whether you can actually see what you're doing in the dark is another story.

I boarded at a barn where they had one of these "lit" arenas. This arena was about 80 x 160 feet and had one power pole on one end with a light on it. When it was turned on, I could barely see more than 60 feet into the arena. Plus the arena had hog fuel which absorbed every bit of available light to boot. Trying to do anything in these conditions was as good as impossible and after a couple of attempts I didn't bother going out at night anymore.

I have also seen a configuration where the arena is directly adjacent to the length of the barn. The lights were attached to the side of the barn and therefore provided light only to that side of the arena.

For an arena to be useful you need a good distribution of light which means that you need light sources all the way around. If you want to jump or do anything serious you need to be able to see what you're doing.

The footing is also a consideration. Since hog fuel is dark, it absorbs light rather than reflect. Shadows are difficult to see as well. Sand, on the other hand, will reflect and appear a lot brighter at night making it a much better combination.

Things to Observe ...

— *Are lights evenly distributed so you can see what you're doing regardless of where you are within the arena?*

— *What kind of footing is used?*

— *Will it reflect light or is it dark and absorbent?*

▼ *You can do SO much fun stuff with barrels that they are definitely at the top of my list of arena toys!*

HOW TO FIND TROUBLE FREE HORSE BOARDING

6. Arena toys...
What are the favorites?

I remember that when I stayed at my friends, they had all the jump standards and poles I could ever desire. I never realized how good I had it until I moved. How do you mean you don't have this kind of stuff? I was really disappointed to find out that they simply had no jumping aids at all.

At that time I wasn't so handy with the power tools as I am today so building these things myself didn't even enter my mind. From that disappointment I certainly learned to make sure that I have plenty of toys at my barn for the boarders to play with. And if I had to see if a boarding place was fun for me, the "toy section" of the arena would be high on my list of things to check.

Toys can include anything from barrels, cones, jumps, poles, cavelettis, dressage letters, tarps, pool noodles, hoola hoops, large balls, cows, you name it. I like to make my horse's life interesting and expose him to lots of different things. It builds his confidence and our relationship. After all, I could wish for nothing more than him seeing me as the coolest horse in his life!

When checking out the toy section, make sure you ask the barn owner about whether other boarders use these too and what the favorites are. Though there may be barn rules in place that request that any jumps or other things are put away after use, you can count on this not happening.

The smaller the item, the likelier it is that they will be put away. But if the majority of the boarders like to jump for example, and the rules are not constantly enforced, you can be sure that the jumps will stay in the arena for the next person to use. It's a lot of work to put them up, and taking them down after an hour of solid riding is even more exhausting. And if the next person is going to use it anyway, why would you?

Enforcing these kinds of barn rules is difficult and exhausting. Plus it doesn't make for a fun atmosphere for anyone involved, not for those doing the enforcing and not for those having to listen. If the barn harrows the arenas at the end of each day, it will be easier to get people to put the toys away, but even then. If you like to do dressage this can get really irritating since you'd be maneuvering through the forever obstacle course. And why should YOU have to put the stuff away? This is another reason why it's a good idea to pick a group of people that have similar interests.

Alternatively, if the facility is large enough, they may have an outdoor arena set up with permanent jumps or perhaps they have a separate dressage arena. Ask the barn owner how they deal with these kinds of issues. If you don't choose wisely, these types of situations can make you stop doing the things that you thought were fun for you.

Questions to Ask ...

— *Would they allow you to bring some of your own favorite toys?*

— *What do most people like to use?*

— *Do jumps get put away or do they have a tendency to stay in the arena?*

Things to Observe ...

— *Is there a "toy" section close to the arena?*

— *Do you see the kind of things you'd like to use?*

3

PART THREE
Make Your Move

HOW TO FIND TROUBLE FREE HORSE BOARDING

CHAPTER 8
Make Your Decision
and Get Ready for Your Move

Looking at all those different places I find in one respect exciting, but also exhausting.

Gathering information, mulling things over, having to make compromises and making decisions based on compromises is not an easy job.

And what about all the associated worries of "I like this but will my horse be okay?", "I saw that one girl dealing with that horse and I wasn't so keen on the way that was handled. Where was the barn owner?"; "For the most part that property looked ok, but that fencing and the way they were putting it up in the midst of the horses was worrisome." This is a tough decision, period.

I hope you had a friend come along for the ride. It just makes the whole deal so much more fun and less stressful, plus you can compare notes at the end of the day over a good dinner and a glass of wine – ok, beer if you prefer.

Which boarding facility stood out from the rest? Can you afford that one? It becomes more of an adventure this way rather than a job. If you have used the work sheets in my work book or you created your own version, you'll have a way to compare the places you went to visit to your own "must haves" and "nice to haves" and build your short list.

If you end up with a couple of favorites, it's time to recheck your budget. Make sure that the extra charges, if there are any, don't put you over the edge. Also don't forget to include your travel time and distance and therefore associated costs for gas and maintenance on your car. Just this last summer gas prices alone went up from $1 per liter to $1.50. That's a 50% increase in cost! Scary. So make sure this is included in your budget.

Then plan on revisiting the facilities, but this time, if it's a public place show up un-announced during their busy time or if it's a private facility, ask whether there would be an issue with you showing up during the time when they feed, turn out, and clean the facilities.

Still like what you see?

Apply for board and once you get accepted...

1. Put in your notice...

These are exciting times, seriously! I know that by the time I had made my decision to move, I couldn't wait.

Often you have to give at least 30 days notice, but check the boarding agreement if you have one. I bet it doesn't stipulate that it has to be on the first day of the month like most property rental agreements would do.

If you do want to get your horse out of the current conditions PDQ, you can always give your 30 days and pay the board for that month and just get out. Just be sure to check with the new facility that they can accommodate your horse sooner rather than later.

It certainly has happened to me on more than one occasion where boarders couldn't leave their old place fast enough. In those cases I just pro-rate the month, and if I can, I'd rather accommodate you in getting you to move as soon as possible, because really, it's all about your horse and you have good reasons for wanting to move him.

2. Call your vet and get the health requirements taken care of...

If the new boarding facility requires you to have particular vaccines or tests completed, call your vet and make the appointment to have them done.

If some of the tests are new to you, make sure that you understand some of the consequences. The one that comes to mind in particular is the Coggins test. This one is required almost everywhere and tests for Equine Infectious Anemia, also called swamp fever.

The disease is spread by horse flies but since the disease doesn't live long on the horse fly – maybe as little as 15 to 30 minutes – the horses would have to be in close proximity to each other in order for it to spread. The disease occurs anywhere horse flies live and a horse could be infected without ever showing symptoms. Horses like this are called carriers.

The downside is that there is no vaccine and if your horse was to have a positive test, it would either have to live under strict quarantine conditions or be destroyed. Not a fun thought, and if you've never done a Coggins test on your horse it could be a bit of a stressful time while you wait for the results.

3. Organize any required memberships or insurance policies...

In our area we have to be members of a particular organization before we're allowed to compete and participate in events. This membership includes a 3rd party liability insurance of five million dollars. A lot of boarding facilities around here require their boarders to have this. That's pretty unique to our local community. Your new barn will let you know what you need to have in place.

This is also a good time to double check whether your home owners' insurance will cover your tack. Make sure you read the fine print though. I had one insurance company tell me that my tack was only allowed to be left at the barn for a couple of days at a time. Others will cover your equipment regardless whether it is kept at home or away.

4. Get your care package together for the transition...

Before a new horse comes to my barn I'll ask the owner to write down exactly what their horse is currently being fed; that means not only the type of hay and grain, but also the exact quantities in weight. Supplements need to be included on the list as well.

Often the horses coming in are on different feeds from what I typically carry so I will also ask the owner to bring a one or two week supply of feed for their horse. This then gives me enough time to transition him over and if he has difficulty adjusting, at least I can keep him on his usual food for the first week or so and let him deal with the surroundings first before introducing more change.

At the very least you need to write down exactly what your horse is currently being fed. Have a chat with the barn owner beforehand and see how they want to go about making the changes and whether they'd like you to bring a week's supply of your horse's food.

5. Arrange your arrival time with the new barn...

I have also found the best time to arrive at a barn is when all the major cleaning and feeding activities have died down. By this time the horses are settled into their daily routine and are happily munching their hay or grass.

Depending on how a barn has their activities organized, the barn owner can then also devote their time to you and your horse and help you settle in. Try not to move in the evening. The dark can be upsetting especially with all the new smells and sounds. The more daylight you can give your horse at the new place on moving day, the better I think.

Find out from the barn owner if they have a preferred arrival time for you and see if they will spend some time with you and your horse on that first day.

6. Organize a hauler for the road trip to move your baby...

If you don't have a trailer to move your horse, you'll need to make arrangements with a transport company. Ask the barn owner if they have someone they could recommend to you. Sometimes they have a trailer on site for this purpose and you could make your arrangements directly with them, however, you might want to check on what type of insurance they have in place for hauling your horse.

Some time back I used one company to haul my two horses to a clinic. Right of the bat, the driver and I didn't hit it off. It was my first time having to load and she was quite condescending and rude to me. When I unloaded my horses at the clinic they were both white eyed, scared out of their minds, half their tails was gone plus they were soaking wet!

I could understand my young boy to being nervous but not my seasoned boy. That was a very rough ride and I certainly wasn't happy. Picking a random number out of the phone book definitely can have its consequences.

When you're picking up the phone to check out transport companies one of your first Questions to Ask them is whether they have "live haul" insurance. Live haul insurance will cover things like vet bills in the event of an injury or accidents. Things like "motor truck" or "cargo" insurance won't.

Proper insurance is very expensive and often transport companies are under insured or carry the wrong insurance or no insurance at all. Most will have "motor truck" or "cargo" insurance which typically only covers the portion of the load that is lost or destroyed in transit. If a horse was to be put down, the payout would barely amount to more than "meat prices". Not a pleasant thought when it comes to your dear companion.

Here in British Columbia, Canada, be wary of people advertising themselves as "licensed & insured". There is no such thing as a "license" to haul horses in B.C. When a transport company is properly insured, insurance rates will run close to $10,000 CAD for the year for them.

There is a good reason for hauling rates being what they are, especially with the proper insurance in place. I know we all like to get away with paying less but, like anything, you get what you pay for. If you have a reputable hauler, don't argue with the price. Your horse will be safer for it and you will have peace of mind.

If you're not sure about the credentials of a transport company, make sure you ask how long the driver has been hauling horses and check their references. Also ask if they have a video monitoring system in the truck so they can see what the horses are doing. On longer trips will they make regular stops to check on them? How often are the horses given water or food? Does the driver have a properly stocked First Aid kit on board? Are the horses tied during transit? Why or why not? Is bedding used in the trailer?

Some of the haulers don't like to use bedding as they believe it creates a slippery floor that's difficult to stand on securely. Personally I prefer using bedding since it absorbs the manure and urine and prevents a slippery floor. Experienced haulers that I have dealt with all seem to be using bedding. So, who's right? I guess it really all depends on the individual's experiences so the best thing is to ask, see what kind of answer you get and compare it with the answers you get from the others.

If you have an opportunity to meet the hauler at a pickup or drop off at the barn, check out their trailer. Is the trailer clean or does the manure look old? Do you see any sharp objects sticking out that could possibly injure a horse? Does the trailer look in good repair? Watch how the hauler handles the horses. Do they talk to the horses, and how? If the horse is nervous or upset, how does the handler deal with the horse? How does he lead the horse? Is there respect toward the horse or does he just grab and haul the head around?

On longer trips a conscientious hauler will give you an update on how well your horse travelled, how much he's had to eat and drink, and will let you know of any odd behaviors he may have noticed. If you want to find out how attentive a driver was on a long trip ask them if there is anything you need to know about how your horse travelled?

Another consideration is the trailer configuration. Everyone certainly has their favorites. Here are some things for you to think about though.

My favorite hauler used to own an angle haul which is a very common type of trailer. Over time he learned that horses are much more comfortable traveling in parallel with the direction they travel. And it doesn't matter if the horse faces backward or forward. So, he ended up buying himself, what's called, a head-to-head straight haul and is loving it. This is a very large and spacious trailer that has four stalls, two on either end, and a center section

that can be used for a horse as well. There is a ramp in the middle and also at the back side of the trailer for easy loading.

This trailer gives him lots of flexibility. He can easily remove the dividers between two stalls and create a box stall to accommodate horses who need more space like a mare with foal or a horse with laminitis, for example. He also found that tending to the horses was much easier compared to his old trailer.

Personally, I've had my three Thoroughbreds hauled in one of these and I could see how comfortable the horses were getting into this one. One of my horses in particular was incredibly stressed when I tried loading her into my old and narrow straight haul trailer. Many years ago she apparently had quite the accident to deal with so who can blame her. With the head-to-head she just took her time, walked in on her own quietly and was completely at ease.

Some horses love as much space as they can get, but others will just pace and race around. If your horse ends up pacing around, you simply need dividers to calm them down. Having the flexibility to change the trailer configuration means a lot. If you're serious

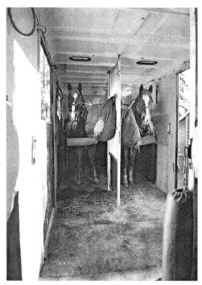

about having a conscientious and professional hauler, make sure you listen to their advice which will be unique to your situation.

◀ *The head-to-head trailer is a nice spacious trailer and offers lots of options. For more pictures and floorplans visit http://h-4.ca/stall.html*

Haulers also put themselves at great risk, so be mindful if they give you specific instructions. But also be clear on the information you give them.

If you have a horse who doesn't tie, LET THEM KNOW! A friend of mine ended up with serious injuries because the owner forgot to tell him that the horse didn't tie.

The trailer is the ultimate CAVE for your horse. Lions live in caves and eat horses. Your horse doesn't know any better! If your horse has ANY issues, no matter how silly you think they may be, please tell the hauler about them. They absolutely NEED TO KNOW since it will help them decide how to approach the situation safely. Also, stay out of the trailer unless you're asked in. My friend ended up with a broken arm because someone wanted to "help".

If you need to pack along a couple of bales of hay and they're not likely to fit in your car, check whether there is room in the trailer for them beforehand, but be specific. Don't say "a few" bales of hay and then show up with 25, 110 lbs bales. They move horses, not cargo. The same goes for tack.

When you've arranged a date and time, make sure your hauler has your contact information. There are times when they can be held up and need to give you a call. It's also useful to have cell phone information if you're travelling together on the road. Quite often you leave together but along the way, traffic may get in the way or you have an unexpected fuel stop. It's handy to have a way of checking in with each other. These things need to be communicated beforehand.

Questions to Ask ...

— *Ask the new barn owner if they trailer horses at all? If not, could they recommend a reputable hauler?*

— *When you're talking to a transport company, ask them*

   ▪ *If they have "live haul" insurance?*

   ▪ *How long has the driver been hauling horses?*

   ▪ *Can they provide any references?*

   ▪ *Do they have a video monitoring system in the truck?*

   ▪ *How often will they stop to check on the horses?*

   ▪ *How often do they give the horses water or food?*

   ▪ *Do they have a stocked First Aid kit on board?*

   ▪ *Are the horses tied during transit? Why or why not?*

   ▪ *Is bedding used in the trailer?*

   ▪ *Will there be space for your tack or extra bales of hay, and if so, how much room is there?*

Things to Observe ...

— *If you get the opportunity, check out the trailer and the handler*

   ▪ *Is the trailer clean or does it look like manure is age old?*

   ▪ *Do you see anything sticking out that your horse could run into and hurt himself on?*

   ▪ *What type of configuration does the trailer have? Would your horse be comfortable in there?*

   ▪ *How does the hauler handle the horses? Do they talk to them and how? How does he lead the horses?*

   ▪ *If the horse is nervous or upset, how does the handler deal with the horse?*

7. Moving day

If the new barn is not far away, your horse can be fed as usual, but if the new facility is a good distance away and requires you to travel 4 to 5 hours or more, make sure your horse doesn't get any grain in the morning. If your horse doesn't travel well, it could promote colic.

Be on time. Not being ready for the agreed upon pickup time can result in extra charges. Also, if you think your horse needs shipping boots, think again. Unless your horse is used to this, it can actually increase their stress levels.

If you were going to bring a week or two supply of his feed, make sure that you have those packed up to go as well. If you're on good terms with the current place you may be able to buy a couple of bales of hay from them and perhaps even the necessary feed.

When the trailer arrives, let the handler load your horse. Once your horse is on, load anything else that's coming along for the trip.

Now you're ready to head on out.

When you arrive at the new barn, the barn owner should show you the way to your horse's new spot. Make sure he has access to hay and water while he starts to look around and check out his new surroundings.

This is a stressful time for him and it's a good time to spend some time with him while he takes in the new smells and sounds. After a while you can take him for a walk and show him some of the property boundaries. Perhaps even meet some of the other horses, but if you do, it would be good to have the barn owner with you. After all, they know the other horses and how they may react to new comers.

HOW TO FIND TROUBLE FREE HORSE BOARDING

CHAPTER 9
Conclusion

Well, we've come to the end of our journey together. I hope you've enjoyed my book and that the information has answered a lot of questions for you. Perhaps it even opened your eyes to things you would never have thought of.

You now know what to look for and what questions to ask to find that **happy, safe** and **healthy** home for your horse and a **fun** place for you!

But don't forget that after you've moved into your new place and you want to keep this a happy place, you need to do your part. Because, when you don't, you not only run the risk that you'll have to move again, but also that your horse could end up paying the price by not getting the care he should be getting as a result of a bad relationship between you and the barn owner. And that's not something we want.

I know, it shouldn't be that way, but unfortunately it does happen.

So, here are some things to keep in mind...

— *Follow the barn rules. Remember, they are there for a good reason.*

— *If you need to break the rules,* **always** *ask for permission first. Nine times out of ten the barn owner will say "yes" simply* **because** *you asked and showed respect.*

— *Clean up after yourself.*

— *Pay your board in full, and on time,* **always***!*

— *Pay your invoices for extras on time.*

— *Keep things in perspective. What you see in the short period of time when you are at the barn is not necessarily representative of what really goes on from day to day. If you're in doubt, talk to the barn owner. Don't be afraid of them.*

— *Work as a team. Don't start complaining that the barn owner isn't doing their job and then not talk to them. Unfortunately, this happens all too often and it doesn't solve anything. Talking behind someone's back doesn't give a person the opportunity to correct a possible problem. Neither is it respectful and if you have a good relationship, it will deteriorate very quickly. And, just because you may not see the barn owner, don't think for a minute that they won't know what is going on.*

— *Be proactive. If there is something you'd like to see cleaned up but it isn't getting done, just pick up the shovel and help out.*

— *Be respectful of the barn owner's time. Remember, you are at the barn on leisure time, but the barn owner is working and earning a living. Just like you are when you go to work.*

I Want to Hear from You!

I would love to hear from you, and especially, I'd like to know:

- Where you were at before you bought my book... what were your fears, frustrations and results you were looking for?
- What did you learn from the book and did the information make a difference in the way you decided on a boarding stable?
- Did you end up getting what you were looking for?
- Do you have an experience that you think someone else could learn from?
- Is there anything that you think should be added to the book to make it even better?

If there is good information that can be added to the book or website, I will take the pieces that fit. I may even touch base with you for clarification. Some of the information you provide may also be used as a testimonial.

Email me your thoughts, questions, and stories at
Ronaye@HorseBoardingSecrets.com

And don't forget to visit my website and blog at
HorseBoardingSecrets.com.

And, Lastly, I have a Free Gift for You

As a "thank you" for buying my book, I have a special gift for you that will help you in your journey. Go to http://horseboardingsecrets.com/trouble-free-horse-boarding/free-gift/ and follow the instructions to claim your free gift.

With love

CPSIA information can be obtained at www.ICGtesting.com
Printed in the USA
LVOW102220191212

312486LV00005B/17/P

9 781933 817651